HARVARD HISTORICAL STUDIES

PUBLISHED UNDER THE DIRECTION OF
THE DEPARTMENT OF HISTORY

FROM THE INCOME OF
THE HENRY WARREN TORREY FUND

VOLUME LXXIV

The Ralliement
in French Politics

1890-1898

ALEXANDER
SEDGWICK

HARVARD UNIVERSITY PRESS

Cambridge, Massachusetts

1965

TO CHARLENE M. SEDGWICK

PREFACE

 In most histories of the Third Republic the *Ralliement* is described as an attempt by the Vatican to persuade French Catholics to accept the Republic. However, it was much more than that. The *Ralliement* represented an effort on the part of French Royalists, Bonapartists, and Opportunists to change their political habits by joining together to form a conservative party within the constitutional framework of the Republic. It was part of a movement in the 1890's to polarize French political activity into what has been called a *parti de l'ordre* and a *parti de mouvement,* the first of a number of unsuccessful attempts by the Right and the Left under the Third Republic to organize homogeneous majorities.

This, then, is a study of French conservative politics in the 1890's. It is not a study of Liberal Catholicism or Social Catholicism as such. When Leo XIII encouraged Cardinal Lavigerie to endorse the Republic in 1890, he was taking advantage of something which had already begun. And although it was in the Vatican's interest to encourage the establishment of a strong government in France backed by a conservative, if Republican, majority, the Pope did not initiate the *Ralliement.* The failure of the anti-Republican Right to overthrow the Republic, the rise of the Socialist party, and the increasing urgency of economic and social problems at the end of the nineteenth century had already made quarrels over constitutional form seem irrelevant.

The *Ralliement* was actually the fifth in a series of unsuccessful attempts by the anti-Republican Right to play an effective role in French politics between 1885 and 1893 after it had become clear that there was virtually no chance of a Bourbon, Orleanist, or Bonapartist restoration. The four efforts which preceded the *Ralliement* included the formation of the *Union des droites* on the eve of the elections in 1885, Raoul-Duval's attempt to create a *Droite républicaine* in 1886–1887, and finally the Conservatives' role in the Boulanger affair of 1888–1889.

The *Ralliement* itself can be divided into two separate phases. The first was dominated by the Conservatives and lasted from 1890 until the elections of 1893, which were ruinous to the Right. Between 1894–1898 French Catholics dominated the movement. Long used to political association with the Conservatives, they realized after 1893 that they were on their own. This accounts for the number of Catholic political organizations which were active between the elections of 1893 and those of 1898.

Those Catholics, Conservatives, and Opportunists who were aware of the need for new political attitudes encountered considerable opposition on the local level. The failure of the *Ralliement* was due, in large part, to the unalterable prejudices of the parish priest who viewed the Republic as the work of the devil, of the *notable* who refused to renounce his cherished belief in a restoration of the monarchy, and of the prefect who was unable to see that times had changed and that anticlericalism was not the issue it had been in the 1870's and the 1880's.

The Dreyfus Affair did not destroy the *Ralliement*. The hopeless divisions within the Right made it impossible for Conservatives to act as a responsible unit in the politics of the 1890's. The movement was destroyed by the refusal of important elements among Catholics, Conservatives, and Republicans to admit that new political attitudes were necessary to cope with the increasing number of social and economic problems confronting France and other nations of the Western World. There was, however, a definite connection between the Dreyfus Affair and the *Ralliement*. For the Affair provided the necessary excuse for intransigent Catholics and Conservatives to reiterate their assertions

that the Republic was dishonorable. It strengthened their conviction that it was impossible to adhere to the Republic and
provided the necessary excuse for many Opportunists and Radicals to revive the old battle cry that the Republic was in danger—
a battle cry which had begun to lose its effectiveness in the 1890's.
In short, the Dreyfus Affair cannot be viewed simply as a victory
of the forces of justice and democracy over the forces of reaction.
It was also a victory of those who refused to abandon obsolete
political habits over those who were prepared to adopt new ones—
namely those who supported the *Ralliement*.

The Panama Scandal and the Dreyfus Affair dominate the
history of France in the 1890's, and to one studying the political
upheavals of this period the *Ralliement* does not appear, at first
glance, to be of great significance. After all, what did it accom-
plish? It failed to bring a substantial number of Conservative
deputies over to the Republic. It also failed to placate the more
vociferous elements of French Catholicism, which continued to
agitate for the revival of the privileged position of the Church
in France until the separation of Church and State in 1905. In
fact, the Panama Scandal and the Dreyfus Affair revealed the
passionate intensity of anti-Republican sentiment which the
Ralliement was unable to overcome.

However, the *Ralliement* was a significant political movement
in that it represented the efforts of Conservatives, Catholics, and
Opportunists to adapt themselves to new conditions. Its failure
provided a striking example of that tradition-bound rigidity in
the political attitudes of so many Frenchmen which, from the
time of the French Revolution to the present, has frustrated the
attempts of the French body politic to meet the challenge of the
moment.

A major difficulty in the study of French political history in
this period is presented by the fact that there were no political
parties as such, only loosely organized parliamentary groups. It
is almost impossible in some instances to determine the affilia-

tions of certain deputies. Given this difficulty I have attempted
to use "party labels" consistently. Thus the label "Conservative"
applies to any deputy who was a member of the *Union des
droites* in the 1880's, and the adjective "conservative" has been
applied to either a member of the Right or to a Republican.
The label "Intransigent" applies to those Conservatives who
refused to accept the *Ralliement*. Finally, the label "Opportunist"
has been applied to the associates and followers of Gambetta
and Jules Ferry. Other historians have called the members of
this group "Progressists" or "Moderates."

Translation always presents problems. In some instances I
have kept the French term or expression. Translation of such
terms as *loi scolaire, loi militaire, droit d'accroissement, Union
des droites, Droite constitutionnelle,* and *Fédération électorale*
is cumbersome. In translating texts I have tried to respect the
integrity of the given text, and in every instance I have respected
the meaning.

This study would not have been possible without the benefit
of two years in France as a Fulbright Scholar which enabled
me to complete the bulk of the research required by the subject,
and which gave me the opportunity to discuss various problems
of church-state relations in France with a number of European
scholars. In this connection I would like to thank Henri Rollet;
the Abbé Charles Molette; Jean-Marie Mayeur of the University
of Strasbourg, who is currently writing a political biography of
the Abbé Lemire; Pierre Guyot de Villeneuve, the grandson of
Jacques Piou; and Canon Roger Aubert of the University of
Louvain, who gave me the benefit of his vast knowledge of the
pontificate of Leo XIII.

I would also like to thank J.-B. Duroselle and more particularly, René Rémond, both of the Institut d'Études Politiques in
Paris, for their assistance in guiding me toward some understanding of the *Ralliement*. David Shapiro of Nuffield College,
Oxford, and H. Stuart Hughes of Harvard University were

more than helpful with their suggestions. I would like to express my particular gratitude to M. Dominique Audollent of Clermont-Ferrand, who gave me permission to examine the papers of Étienne Lamy, of which he is the owner. And the Committee on Research of the University of Virginia very generously financed the typing of the manuscript. Finally, I would like to thank my wife whose help as editor was invaluable.

Alexander Sedgwick
Charlottesville, Virginia
15 June 1964

CONTENTS

The Ralliement
in French Politics

1890–1898

CHAPTER I

Introduction

Leo XIII became Pope on February 20, 1878. It was a difficult time for the Papacy, which was confronted by a unified and hostile Kingdom of Italy and by alien social and political concepts. Leo's predecessor, Pius IX, had stood firm against the Italian government's efforts to annex the Papal States, and when at last Rome itself became the capital of the new kingdom, Pius refused to accept the fact and committed Vatican policy to an unceasing atttempt to regain the lost territory. In his *Syllabus of Errors* (1864) he vigorously opposed the new ideas which pervaded Western thought. Would Leo XIII remain faithful to the policy of Pius IX?

It has been argued that Leo XIII was a liberal, and thoroughly modern.[1] His conciliatory policy toward the Republican government of France, and the great encyclical, *Rerum Novarum* (1891), are cited to support this conclusion, and it is certainly true that many contemporary European statesmen, including Léon Gambetta, one of the founders of the Third Republic, believed that the new pope was amenable to ideas that were current in the nineteenth century.[2] Yet to argue along these lines is to approach the problem in the wrong way.

Leo XIII was as troubled by the isolated position of the Vatican as his predecessor, and he was equally concerned about the prestige of the Church. All his energies were devoted to removing the Vatican from its current isolation and restoring the Catholic Church to its former position of authority. This accounts for his

[1] E. Lecanuet, *L'Église de France sous la Troisième République*, vol. II *Pontificat de Léon XIII, 1878–94* (Paris, 1910), preface.

[2] *Ibid.*, p. 9.

painstaking efforts of diplomacy with regard to the European powers and for his innumerable letters and encyclicals on the role of the Church in society. If his methods were different from those of Pius IX, his goals were the same. Where Pius was rigid and intolerant, Leo was patient and long-suffering.[3]

Nowhere are the efforts and interests of Leo XIII more clearly revealed than in his dealings with France. Republican France was acutely affected by philosophical concepts which were hostile to Catholic doctrine. By making France an ally of the Vatican, Leo XIII would have gone a long way toward ending the Papacy's isolation and reviving the prestige of the Church.

One might well ask why France was singled out by the Pope to receive his special consideration. The European diplomatic situation between 1878 and 1890 from the point of view of the Vatican provides a partial answer. It seemed unlikely that Leo XIII could pin his hopes on the Triple Alliance to restore Rome to the Papacy. Italy was unquestionably hostile, having annexed Rome and the Papal States and having embarked on a program of anticlerical legislation; Vatican relations with Germany were to improve during the decade of the 1880's, after the *Kultur-kampf,* but they never became more than correct; and the Austro-Hungarian Empire, though strongly Catholic, was not prepared to subordinate its foreign policy to the wishes of the Vatican. England and Russia were not Catholic countries, and the Church presented problems for England in Ireland and for Russia in Poland.

France hardly looked promising. The Republicans were extremely hostile to the Church and were enacting legislation de-

---

[3] A definitive history of the pontificate of Leo XIII has yet to be written. Mgr. de T'serclaes, *Le Pape Léon XIII, sa vie, son action religieuse, politique et sociale* (Paris, 1894), 2 vols., is an official biography written in the middle of the pontificate and suffers accordingly from a lack of objectivity. Its value lies in the fact that it is Leo XIII's approved version of Vatican policy from 1878–1894. We must wait, however, for the publication of Canon Roger Aubert's study of the Church under Leo XIII.

signed to limit severely its influence on French society. France had, however, one characteristic in common with the Vatican. She was isolated. Defeated in the Franco-Prussian war, stripped of Alsace and Lorraine, confronted with a new and mighty Germany now more powerful because of the Triple Alliance, France could never hope to recover her lost provinces or her rightful place in the concert of Europe unless she found friends. Her relations with England were poor because of various conflicts in North Africa, and there was little chance of improving them after Britain had virtually annexed Egypt in 1882. France could hardly expect support from Russia in the 1880's because Bismarck had seen to it that Russia and France remained apart. Then too, Tsar Alexander III disliked republics. Italy was a member of the Triple Alliance, and she was in constant conflict with France over Tunisia, which the French had taken over in 1881. Thus if Leo XIII could help France find an ally, the French government might be grateful and return the favor.

In 1889 Isvolsky, Russia's future foreign minister, was sent to the Vatican as ambassador. At that time the Pope was particularly interested in obtaining from the Tsar a promise of better treatment for Polish Catholics. Although little is known of these negotiations, it is certain that various problems connected with France were discussed. It would seem likely that the Vatican was instrumental in creating the climate in which the French fleet was received at Kronstadt in 1891 and in influencing Alexander III to change his views on the Third Republic. The fact that the policy of the *Ralliement,* the improvement of relations between the Vatican and St. Petersburg, the dismissal of Bismarck as chancellor, and the reception at Kronstadt all occurred within a period of two years can hardly be viewed as coincidental.[4]

[4] Analyses of Leo XIII's foreign policy are to be found in T'serclaes, *Le Pape Léon XIII,* I, 498–505; Adrien Dansette, *Histoire religieuse de la France contemporaine* (Paris, 1951), II, 100–105; William L. Langer, *The Franco-Russian*

The desire to create a better diplomatic climate which would ultimately resolve the Roman question does not entirely explain why Leo XIII wanted a reconciliation with France. One of his great concerns was the position and prestige of the Church in a changing world. Reading through his encyclicals one finds that the dominant theme is the maintenance of traditional authority. In his first encyclical, *Inscrutabili* (1878), the Pope deplored ". . . this revolt of the spirit, incapable of accepting any legitimate authority . . ."[5] This was the cause of the present evils in the world. The human mind was rejecting authority, particularly the authority of the Church.

The more the enemies of religion take it upon themselves to instruct ignorant men, and particularly young people, in those things which obscure their vision and corrupt their morals, the more it becomes essential to overcome such teaching by means of a suitable and firm method. This method would involve instruction in the arts and sciences conforming on all points with the doctrine of the Catholic Church, and more particularly in philosophy, which determines to a very large extent the orientation of the other sciences.[6]

This was a call to arms. The Church would combat the errors of the modern world.

In *Rerum Novarum* (1891), often considered to be the most liberal of Catholic utterances in the nineteenth century, one finds the same concern and the same conviction that only through the Church could conflicts between social classes be resolved. Leo XIII attacked socialism because it disturbed the public peace and because it was contrary to natural law.

In his encyclical *Immortale Dei* (1886) on the various types of civil constitutions, the Pope pointed out that the constitution

---

Alliance, 1890–94 (Cambridge, Mass., 1929), pp. 235–237; Jacques Piou, *Questions religieuses et sociales* (Paris, 1910), pp. 11–28; Anonymous, "The Policy of the Pope," *Contemporary Review*, 62:457–477 (October 1892); James E. Ward, "Leo XIII and Bismarck; the Kaiser's Vatican Visit of 1888," *The Review of Politics* (July 1962), XXIV, pp. 392–414.

[5] T'serclaes, *Le Pape Léon XIII*, I, 207.
[6] *Ibid.*, I, 207.

of a given state was unimportant as long as its authority was based on the law of God. "The right to command is not necessarily associated with any particular form of government. But in any government those who govern must respect God, the Supreme Master of the world. Their administrations must reflect this respect." [7]

This obsession with order and obedience was a leading factor in Leo XIII's particular concern for France. In the encyclical *Nobilissima Gallorum gens* (1884), addressed to the people of France, the Pope insisted that the country's difficulties were caused by an immoderate spirit of liberty, as well as by secret societies such as the Freemasons, which thrived on the oppression of the Church. He pointed out that "there can be no prosperity in a state where religion has been extinguished," and that for Christian nations as well as for individuals "it is as salutary to submit to the designs of God as it is dangerous not to heed them." [8]

The world was in great danger of destruction because Christian nations paid no attention to the law of God as interpreted by the Holy Catholic Church. This point of view was hardly different from that taken by the doctrinaire Pius IX. But where Pius remained aloof and isolated from the world around him, Leo came to grips with it. The successors of St. Peter could not withdraw into the Castel Sant'Angelo while the enemies of Christendom were on the rampage. The Church Militant had to go forth and reconquer what had been taken from it.

The condition of the French Church was a third reason for Leo XIII's interest in French politics. The welfare of the Church in France was of great importance to Catholicism not only because of its potential influence in a great power, but also because of the number of French missionaries throughout the world.

[7] *Ibid.*, I, 211.
[8] *Ibid.*, I, 311–312.

The Pope deplored the anticlerical spirit which seemed to dominate the actions of the Republican government toward the Church and wanted to do everything in his power to ameliorate the situation. His strong feelings on the subject were reflected in a letter which he wrote to President Jules Grévy on May 12, 1883. He complained that the conciliatory attitude of the Vatican toward the French government since 1878 had not been reciprocated:

> Such an attitude on the part of the Holy See gave us the right to hope that the government of the Republic, in its turn, would pursue a benevolent and amicable policy with regard to the Catholic Church by applying toward it those principles of true liberty which all wise and enlightened governments are proud to have as a basis for policy.[9]

In the letter the Pope enumerated the grievances of the French Church, with particular reference to the elimination of the role of the Church in primary education. In *Nobilissima Gallorum gens* (1884), Leo XIII again complained of the government's policy toward the Church as a violation of the Concordat of 1801. He extolled the Concordat as an ideal expression of temporal and spiritual relations. Worried by the desire of some Republicans to separate church and state, he felt it his duty to save the Concordat and to see that it was justly applied.

Leo XIII was also disturbed by the divisions among French Catholics. The nineteenth century struggles between the Liberals led by Lammenais, Montalembert and Lacordaire and the Intransigents led by Louis Veuillot; the ancient conflict of Gallicans and Ultramontanes; these had left their scars on the French Church. Further persecution by Republican governments might be disastrous. The Pope believed that the lack of unity in the Church encouraged her enemies.

Rather than hurl anathemas at the Republicans, Leo decided early in his pontificate to adopt a policy of appeasement toward the French government. There were a number of advantages to

[9] T'serclaes, *Le Pape Léon XIII*, I, 301.

such a policy. It might free the Church from anticlerical attacks, thereby reducing the tension among French Catholics, and it might also cause a Republican government to be more favorably disposed toward the Vatican. In 1879 the Pope sent Monsignor Czacki to Paris as nuncio, with Dominique Ferrata, the future nuncio during the period of the *Ralliement,* as auditor. Czacki took the position that the Republic was the *de facto* government, if nothing else, and for that reason had to be respected.[10] Furthermore he felt that the Monarchists were using the religious question for their own political ends and that this was detrimental to the Church. In October 1879 Czacki approached the Marquis de Dreux-Brézé, the Comte de Chambord's representative to the Royalist political committees in France, in order to get him to persuade the Pretender that it was pointless to oppose the Republic, which was now firmly established. He insisted that the Royalists could find a fruitful terrain for political action only on the grounds of protecting the interests of the Church. Unable to convince Dreux-Brézé, the Nuncio sought out another of the Comte de Chambord's representatives, M. de Blacas, who took Czacki's suggestions to Frohsdorf and returned a few weeks later with the Pretender's classic reply: "I always thought that the Church forbade suicide." [11]

On March 29, 1880, the Freycinet ministry issued decrees dissolving all religious orders which failed to obtain permission from the government to continue in existence. This presented the Vatican with an opportunity to reiterate its policy of conciliation. Using Cardinal Lavigerie as the intermediary between Rome and Paris, Leo XIII reached an agreement with Freycinet whereby all the Orders (excluding the Jesuits) would take an oath of loyalty to the Republic in which they would declare their political neutrality. This agreement was foiled by the

---

[10] Dominique Ferrata, *Ma Nonciature en France* (Paris, Action Populaire, 1922), p. 38.

[11] Lecanuet, *L'Église de France,* II, 170–171.

machinations of the Royalists, who opposed any conciliation between the Church and the Republic.[12]

A number of other instances, including Leo XIII's letter to President Grévy (cited above) and *Nobilissima Gallorum gens,* show clearly that the Pope was anxious to gain the good will of the French government. This desire, inspired by three considerations—the diplomatic isolation of the Vatican, the restoration of spiritual authority in the modern world and the grievous position and condition of the Church in France—ultimately led in 1890 to the *Ralliement.*

Why wasn't the *Ralliement* initiated in the 1880's? The answer to this lies in an analysis of the politics of the French Right and the Republicans in this period. In order to draw Catholics to the Republic, an opportune moment would have to be found when the Right would accept and further the movement and when the Republicans would be receptive to it. But before attempting such an analysis, a closer look must be taken at the Church in France upon which the success or failure of the *Ralliement* would ultimately depend.

The divisions within the Catholic Church in France have been mentioned. Throughout the nineteenth century Gallican fought Ultramontane, and Liberal fought Intransigent. The great leaders of the Church, Louis Veuillot, Bishop Dupanloup, and Montalembert, devoted most of their energies to internecine struggles. In the period of the 1880's these struggles were less apparent because the attention of the Church was drawn to its conflict with the state. Yet they existed, and they were to flare up again during the period of the *Ralliement.* In a letter addressed to the foreign minister, Freycinet, and dated January 1, 1886, Lefebvre de Béhaine, French ambassador to the Holy See, wrote:

Some [Catholics] spend their time looking for vague and flexible formulas with which to relieve tension between the temporal and the

---

[12] J. Tournier, *Le Cardinal Lavigerie et son action politique 1863-92* (Paris, 1913), pp. 94-95.

spiritual, thereby allowing them to take their rightful places in governing circles. Others continue to believe that it is necessary to maintain doctrinal purity. While rendering unto Caesar that which is Caesar's, questions touching the doctrine of the faith should remain beyond Caesar's jurisdictional competence.[13]

There were other sources of division among French Catholics. Léon de Cheyssac, in his book on the *Ralliement,* explained the movement as a necessary reaction on the part of the Vatican against the Gallicanism which still existed in France despite the triumph of ultramontanism at the Vatican Council of 1869–1870.[14]

French Catholics, laymen and clerics alike, reacted violently to what they considered to be unwarranted encroachments on the part of the government in areas of Church interest, particularly in the field of education. They feared that the complete removal of religious influence from the primary school would be detrimental to the social order. Therefore they fought the Republicans bitterly on such issues as education and divorce, and here they found that they were able to make common cause with the anti-Republican parties. The desire to combat the anti-clericalism fundamental to the Republican ideal was one of the chief reasons why French Catholics and Conservatives were indissolubly allied in the early decades of the Third Republic.

It was true that many bishops sympathized with the Royalist cause, some like De Cabrières of Montpellier because they came from Royalist families,[15] others because of a natural coincidence of interests. But with few exceptions they respected the established order, and they accepted its authority. Only in areas where they felt that the state had no jurisdictional competence did they offer resistance. This point is made again and again in contemporary reports on the state of the clergy at the end of the nineteenth century. Speaking of the French bishops who were in Rome for the celebrations of the tenth anniversary of the pontifi-

---

[13] Archives Nationales (hereinafter cited as A. N.) F19 1943.
[14] Léon de Cheyssac, *Le Ralliement* (Paris, 1906), p. 8.
[15] E. Lecanuet, *La Vie de l'église sous Léon XIII* (Paris, 1930), p. 96.

cate of Leo XIII, Lefebvre de Béhaine in a letter to Flourens, the French Foreign Minister, wrote:

I must add that during their sojourn in Rome our bishops in general went to great pains to make known their feelings of respect toward the government. All who came to see me at the Rospigliosi Palace made it clear that they were very anxious to remain on good terms with the civil authorities. The heads of our most important dioceses undertook to convince me that the Church and the Republic could live in harmony as long as religious interests were not made the objects of the outrageous attacks which have so disconcerted Catholics during the past few years.[16]

And in a report drawn up for the Ministry of Public Worship on July 24, 1888 the Procurator-General of Aix-en-Provence quoted Archbishop Gouthe-Soulard, who was to cause trouble for the *Ralliement* in 1891, as follows:

We must fight! A Christian education is of the utmost importance. The priests must devote all their energies to diminishing the evil done by the atheist schools.

Having trumpeted forth this call to action, the Archbishop went on to say that

. . . the Church must tolerate the Republicans and the Republic. She must accept certain facts while maintaining the purity of her ideal.[17]

The bishops on the whole were willing to live peacefully within the framework of the Republic if the Republic would respect the rights of the Church. For this reason they professed obedience to the established authority while attacking the "laic laws." They accepted the form but not the substance of the Republic. The substance of the Republic, in their minds, consisted of the men and ideals of the Third Republic. This was to explain to a large extent their attitude during the 1890's.

If the cardinals, archbishops, and bishops were on the whole

[16] A. N. F19 1943.
[17] A. N. F19 5610.

moderate in their attitude toward the state, the parish priests were more fanatic. There are a number of reasons for this. The education that they received in the seminaries did little to equip them to cope with the modern world. They read nothing but seventeenth-century authors or diocesan weeklies, which isolated them from current problems. The methods that they had been taught were designed to refute Voltaire, but not Renan.[18] This isolation, caused by an inadequate education, was a chief factor in the loss of respect that the village priest suffered and was the reason why an increasing number of people abandoned the Church even in traditionally strong Catholic areas.[19]

It is often the case that political passions are most acute at the local or "grass-roots" level. This was certainly true in the struggle between the Church and the Third Republic. The *curés* were the ones who suffered most from the laic legislation in the 1880's. They were being denied their traditional role as the local representatives of moral authority by the Republic. The village schoolmaster, often ardently anticlerical, was bent on undermining religious influence, as were the prefects and subprefects. In 1890 few *curés* felt that they could make peace with the schoolmasters. Even when their bishops counseled them to be moderate in their actions, many priests defied or misconstrued the advice. In his report of July 3, 1888, on the state of the clergy, drawn up for the Ministry of Public Worship, the Procurator-General of Agen wrote of the moderate bishop of Auch's relations with his clergy: "Thus his advice and recommendations have no effect, particularly during election time." This hostility toward Republicans held true for the Christian Democrats as well. Men like the Abbé Garnier and the Abbé Gayraud, who enthusiastically endorsed the principles of democracy and who saw the need for bringing the Church in line with the times,

---

[18] Dansette, *Histoire religieuse*, II, 23.
[19] P. C. Berthout, "Le clergé français et le peuple à la fin du XIXe siècle," *Revue du Clergé Français*, 18:25–46 (March 1899).

refused to be conciliatory toward the Republicans in power. A survey of the French clergy taken by *Le Figaro* (November 16, 1891) revealed that most priests were hostile toward the Republic. This attitude contributed to the failure of the *Ralliement,* and it explains the enthusiasm with which parish priests adopted the Boulanger cause in 1889.[20]

2

The elections of 1881 indicated that Royalists and Bonapartists as such could do nothing to bring down the Republic. This was the last election in which both groups were to plead their respective causes before the voters. The result was a drastic reduction in the number of right-wing seats in the Chamber. There were now only ninety-six where before the elections there had been approximately 164.[21] The Bonapartists at this time were in a sorry condition. The Prince Imperial had been killed in Africa in 1878 while serving with the British army, and his followers had divided their allegiance between Prince Jerome Bonaparte and his son, Victor. This in itself weakened the Imperialist cause considerably.

The Monarchists (Legitimists and Orleanists) had patched up their differences when the Orleanist Pretender, the Comte de Paris, recognized the Comte de Chambord, grandson of the last Bourbon king, Charles X, as the true claimant to the throne. Chambord in turn had accepted the Comte de Paris as his successor. But when the Comte de Chambord died in 1883, discouragement was rampant among the Monarchists. Some Legitimists (a small minority, to be sure) ignored the provisions of the Treaty of Utrecht of 1714 and shifted their allegiance to the Spanish Bourbons. They would not accept as heir to the throne the descendant of the regicide Philippe Égalité.

[20] A. Daniel, *L'Année politique,* 1889, p. 186.
[21] Charles Seignobos, *L'Évolution de la Troisième République* (Paris, 1921), p. 82.

The question in the minds of many Conservatives after the elections of 1881 was whether they could survive politically. Divided as they were in 1881, there seemed to be little hope for them. What would happen if they put aside their differences, which were chiefly dynastic, and united on common ground? If they united, should it be within the framework of the Republic, under the Church or merely on the basis of common issues without reference to the constitutional question at all? Throughout the period 1885–1893, Conservatives cast about to find a solution to the problem of effective political unity. And although they had little difficulty in finding common issues, such as the defense of the Church or the budget, they were never able to agree on how to dispose of the constitutional question. Between 1885 and 1893 there were five attempts on the part of Conservatives to organize in such a way as to appeal to the electorate effectively.

In 1885 the need for unity was squarely presented in a pamphlet entitled *Le parti conservateur et son avenir* written by a Monarchist, Rémy de Simony. Monarchists must unite with all Conservatives "regardless of personalities or flags." He said:

Are not all Conservatives in agreement as to the politics of the present government? Is there any among them who approved of Article Seven, the decrees against the religious orders, the forced laicization of the schools, the purging of the administrative cadres, the republicanization of the magistracy, Republican finances or the government's railroad policy . . . ? Is there any among them who finds this sort of thing suitable to the prestige of the country, amenable to her internal pacification, to the rebuilding of her strength and to the augmentation of her financial resources? Here is a complete program furnished by the government itself to a potentially effective party.[22]

Unity became even more desirable for the Conservatives as the differences between the Republican Opportunists and Radicals increased. Aware of this, seventy-six of the ninety-six Conserva-

[22] Henri Rémy de Simony, *Le parti conservateur et son avenir* (Lille, 1885), pp. 40, 67.

tive deputies in the Chamber banded together into a *Union des droites* in 1885. Their program was similar to that presented by Rémy de Simony. It protested against the policies of the government, its "deficit, violence, religious persecution, its failure to respect the rights of families . . ."[23] Nothing was said about restoration or a revision of the constitution. The result was that on the first ballot 176 Conservatives were elected, as opposed to 127 Republicans. Only an appeal for Republican unity on the second ballot prevented the Republicans from being routed. The new Chamber consisted of 383 Republicans and 201 Conservatives.[24] The Conservatives had proved that they were more effective when they avoided the constitutional question and discussed issues. As the Comte de Paris himself wrote after the elections:

> You [Conservatives] succeeded on the first ballot because you were united and you were prudent. Remain united and prudent! Form yourselves into a single unit similar to the "Tories" and the "Whigs." Do not call yourselves anything provocative. Better something neutral so that various shades of conservative opinion will be able to join the group. This is true union for action.[25]

After the elections the *Union des droites* continued to function on a loosely organized basis. It had three presidents—one Monarchist, one Bonapartist, and one Conservative with no particular allegiance. It sought to present a united front on religious and political questions debated in the Chamber. Alarmed by the popularity of Boulanger among the Radicals and the *revanchiste* spirit of the Left in 1886 and 1887, the *Union des droites* attempted to reach an agreement with the Opportunists. The Baron de Mackau, the leading figure in the group, called on President Grévy on May 24, 1887, to say that the Right on the whole would support a moderate government. Grévy asked

[23] Seignobos, *L'Évolution de la Troisième République*, p. 115.
[24] *Ibid.*, pp. 115–117.
[25] Jacques Piou, *Le Comte Albert de Mun, sa vie publique* (Paris, 1919), p. 89.

Rouvier, a banker with connections in the world of high finance, to form a ministry, and De Mackau, Paul de Cassagnac, the Marquis de Ferronays and Jacques Piou tried to come to terms with him. These leaders of the *Union des droites* asked for a more tolerant attitude on the part of the government toward the clergy and the nonauthorized monastic orders and a letup in the laicization of primary schools still run by the religious orders. They also asked for a rigorously controlled budget and the cessation of public works projects. The Conservatives claimed that they received a written statement from Rouvier agreeing in the main to these proposals. Rouvier denied that any agreement had been made.[26]

The attempt of the Conservatives to bargain with the Opportunists showed that the Right was willing to negotiate with the party in power instead of bitterly opposing the regime, as it had done rather unsuccessfully between 1878 and 1885. It indicated that the Conservatives were jockeying for position and trying to utilize their increased strength in the Chamber more effectively. However, by refusing to accept the constitution, the bargaining power of the Right was limited. Was it politically feasible to continue to avoid the constitutional question?

Albert de Mun, one of the great Catholic leaders of the nineteenth century, felt that acceptance of the constitution could be avoided without sacrificing effectiveness. Like so many legitimists, he recognized the fact that with the death of the Comte de Chambord in 1883 the chances of a restoration were negligible, but he considered the cause of the Church in itself reason enough to remain in politics. De Mun agreed with other Conservatives that the key to political success was concerted action. Before the elections of 1885, he and twelve others launched an appeal to all Catholics to unite in defense of the Church. But

[26] *Ibid.*, p. 90. See also Seignobos, *L'Évolution de la Troisième République,* pp. 124–127; François Goguel, *La Politique des partis sous la Troisième République,* 3rd ed. (Paris, 1957), pp. 61–62.

because it was made just before the elections, with little organization behind it, this appeal was not particularly effective.[27]

After the elections De Mun set about forming what he called a *Parti catholique* based upon principles which he laid down in a letter to Admiral Gicquel des Touches written on August 28, 1885:

I desire that all Catholics come to the defense of the Church convinced as I am that it is a legitimate cause. Putting aside petty political differences, they must direct all their efforts toward that defense. This would give all Conservatives who are buffeted about by the tempest created by the social question a great issue, which they have lacked up to now . . . The Revolution is bankrupt. This has never appeared more clearly than in the legislature whose term is now coming to an end.

After a sharp attack on Republican policies, De Mun went on to say:

I would like to see a party rise out of these agitations which would put the question frankly on this ground [i.e., the defense of the Church] addressing itself to the people of the cities, of the factories, and of the country, showing them on the one hand the Revolution, their true enemy, which has tantalized them for over a century with chimerical promises, never offering them a remedy or a relief from suffering, offering them no other recourse but hate, and on the other the Church, their natural protector, offering them repose, concord and stability in the legislation and institutions inspired by its teachings, and protection from abuse in the patronage of the upper classes enlightened by its doctrines.

In a letter to Vicomte Louis de Bélizal on October 30, 1885, De Mun sought to ward off the possible objection that the Catholic party might run counter to other political interests of the Conservatives: "The constitution of the Parliamentary group would not divide the Conservative minority but would unite it more effectively . . ."[28]

[27] Henri Rollet, *Albert de Mun et le parti catholique* (Paris, 1947). This monograph presents a detailed account of the short-lived *parti catholique*.
[28] *Ibid.,* pp. 42, 43, 63.

The difference between the *Parti catholique* and the *Union des droites* lay in the fact that De Mun's group offered a more concrete basis for action. The Count's assumption was that most Frenchmen were practicing Catholics, and that if a political party could associate itself with the influence of the Church, such an association would provide both strength and popularity. De Mun was very much impressed by the Center party in Germany and the Liberal party in Belgium, whose strength resided in their close ties with the Church.

The *Parti catholique* ran into solid opposition both from the Conservative leaders and from the Vatican. From the Conservative point of view, De Mun's party threatened to divide rather than unite the Right. Many felt that the social ideas of the Count were too radical and that they ran counter to material interests. Another objection was that a Catholic party would stimulate the Republicans to enact further anticlerical legislation. At the same time, a Catholic party would automatically invite clerical interference in elections, and this would not be in accord with the provisions of the Concordat. For these reasons only thirty-five of the 201 Conservative deputies adhered to De Mun's group.

The Vatican's objections were similar to those of De Mackau and other leaders of the Right. Leo XIII was very much influenced by Cardinal Lavigerie, Primate of North Africa, who had become convinced of the need for a rapprochement between the French Church and the government. The Cardinal opposed De Mun's organization because it was too "Catholic" and for that reason likely to provoke the government of the Republic to further hostile action. In a letter to the papal Secretary of State dated November 11, 1885 he wrote:

Opinions which are attributed to M. de Mun, his political associations with the late Comte de Chambord, and his intransigent Conservative position in general are likely to prejudice and repel a large segment of neutral public opinion. Most Frenchmen would look unsympathetically upon any association formed and directed by him.

This is immediately apparent in the strong opposition of the Conservative press to his enterprise . . . De Mun's idea is dangerous for two reasons: first, it would be looked upon as a declaration of war by Catholics on what are known today as "modern ideas" and would cause the government to act against the Church with impunity; secondly, fresh divisions among Catholics would weaken our cause, and perhaps inflict a mortal wound upon it.[29]

The Vatican condemned the movement, and on November 9, 1885, De Mun dissolved his Catholic party which had lasted barely three months.

Another attempt to revamp Conservative forces was made by Raoul-Duval, a disillusioned Bonapartist deputy. On August 29, 1886, he wrote to fellow-Bonapartist, Lucien Millevoye, about the need for concerted action, drawing attention to what he considered to be a serious weakness in the *Union des droites.* The letter was published some years later, during the first phase of the *Ralliement,* in *La France Nouvelle* (March 22, 1891).

Intelligent Royalists as well as Bonapartists are forced to realize that neither would yield to the other on the question of dynasties if the Conservatives were to obtain a majority . . . They would do exactly the same thing as the Monarchists of the National Assembly [1871–1876] did, which was to accept the Republican form . . .

Raoul-Duval believed that if the Right accepted the Republic, it would attract a number of voters who had hitherto voted for Opportunists.

On November 6, 1886, Raoul-Duval made a speech in the Chamber in which he stated that conservative ideals could be maintained only within the framework of the Republic. The internal situation in France needed immediate attention if the nation was not to succumb to the socialist menace. He emphasized that the Republic could be made to serve conservative interests, as Thiers had wished. France would be far better off if the voter were offered a choice between two great parties. The

---

[29] Henri Rollet, *Albert de Mun et le parti catholique* (Paris, 1947), p. 71.

essence of this speech was contained in the phrase, "Une droite dans la République et non contre la République." (*La Droite Républicaine,* January 9, 1887).

La Droite Républicaine, a newspaper dedicated to the propagation of Raoul-Duval's ideas, began publication on November 14, 1886. Its editorials stressed the socialist menace and the need to defend France against it. According to *La Droite Républicaine* (December 5, 1886), the best defense lay in an alliance between the upper class and the bourgeoisie, which was, in the last analysis, conservative.

. . . we are certain that it is the Bourgeoisie alone which is capable of making the Republic last. History has shown us that the bloody and demagogic orgies of '93 compromised the work of '89; socialist pretensions of 1848 destroyed the Second Republic. The Third Republic will perish for the same reason if help doesn't come to it from above, that is to say from the ranks of the Conservatives.

Raoul-Duval's movement evoked little response among Conservatives. Many Monarchists and Bonapartists found it impossible to make a formal adherence to the Republic.

The bases of our Union are always readily apparent; the defense of Catholic interests, the vindication of all religious and civil liberties, and the defense of material interests. But if our immediate aim is the defense of Conservative principles our ultimate aim is the Restoration.

This statement of the Duc de la Rochefoucauld, which appeared in *La Droite Républicaine* on January 9, 1887, presents the thinking of the intransigent Monarchists and Bonapartists in the clearest possible light. In their innermost thoughts there always remained the possibility of a restoration, and belief in this possibility was sacred, even though they discussed other more pressing matters before the voters. Here they differed from the Conservatives who followed Raoul-Duval and who believed that social and economic questions were so compelling that dynastic interests should be laid aside forever. The followers of Raoul-Duval were convinced that they had to accept the Republic in order to protect their interests. The difference between the two groups was irremediable and forced the latter to turn from right to left. In the final issue of the short-lived *Droite Républicaine* which appeared on March 13, 1887, the editors took pains to point out that the differences between themselves and the Opportunists were minimal.

Raoul-Duval had few followers. The most important among them was Francis Magnard, editor of *Le Figaro,* who from that time on dedicated his paper to the cause of constitutional conservatism. Raoul-Duval himself died in February 1887, and his movement sank rapidly into oblivion, aided no doubt by Boulangism, which attracted so many Conservatives. The movement did, however, foreshadow the first phase of the *Ralliement*.

The appeal that Boulanger had for many members of the *Union des droites* is explained by the unceasing efforts of the Conservatives to find an effective means of furthering their cause. They had rejected the approaches of De Mun and of Raoul-Duval. Boulanger, on the other hand, was popular, and he opposed the regime. Boulangism gave the Conservatives an opportunity to present their grievances under the aegis of a popular hero and also offered the possibility of an eventual restoration. As the Comte de Paris wrote in a circular of April 24, 1888:

Nothing is more just than to insist on the dissolution of a discredited Chamber and on the revision of the Constitution . . . Conservatives must demand revision from the Nation loyally consulted and not from its faction-ridden Parliament.[30]

Practically all the leaders of the Right, including the Comte de Paris and Prince Victor Bonaparte, joined in the cause. The central committee was made up of De Mackau, De Beauvoir, De Cassagnac, De Breteuil, De Mun, and Jacques Piou. The last two were to become leaders of the *Ralliement*. Thus the machinery of the *Union des droites* was committed to Bou-

[30] Daniel, *L'Année politique,* p. 139.

langism even though not all of the Right went along with the movement. The Conservatives in the Senate were opposed, as well as leading newspapers such as *Le Soleil, Le Moniteur Universel,* and the *Gazette de France.* Their main objection was that General Boulanger was too closely associated with the Radicals. However, as the historian, Adrien Dansette, points out, "Thanks to the influence which it maintained in the country and the financial support it brought to Boulanger, the Royalist party was the most important element in the Boulanger movement . . ." [31]

The behavior of the Right between 1885 and 1889 seems inconsistent and can only be understood if one keeps in mind its desperate attempts to find some basis for effective political action. The key to such action was unity, and Baron de Mackau wrote in a pamphlet entitled *L'Union, préface de la victoire* (published in 1889), "Unity has been your program, your true program." He appealed to the Conservatives to "gather in all the truly conservative elements and unite them against the faction which maintains power and exploits it." But it was difficult to get all Conservatives to agree on a common approach. The best that could be achieved, given the differences of opinion in the 1880's, was the loosely organized *Union des droites.*

3

In 1877 the Republic was definitely established. The Republicans controlled majorities in the Chamber and in the Senate, and Jules Grévy, a Republican, had replaced Marshal MacMahon as President. However there arose considerable differences of opinion among the three hundred Republicans in the Chamber as to whether the Republic should be conservative, moderate, or radical, and between 1879 and 1893 there were three separate groups within the Republican majority.

On the right were the Left-Centrists who had broken from

[31] Adrien Dansette, *Le Boulangisme* (Paris, 1928), p. 184.

the Right over the constitutional question in 1875. They were led by Léon Say (son of the classical economist Jean-Baptiste Say), who was closely associated with the Rothschild enterprises; Jules Simon, whose career as a Republican extended back to 1848; and Henri Bardoux, a distinguished lawyer. The group included some Catholics such as Edouard de Marcère and Étienne Lamy, but these failed to be re-elected in 1881 because they opposed Republican policy toward the Church. The rest supported the government, except for its anticlerical program, until 1885; they then went into opposition because of its fiscal policy. The Left-Centrists were staunchly conservative in economic matters, and their election manifesto of 1885 accused the government of economic irresponsibility, which they regarded as the cause of political instability and the ruin of the country.[32]

The Left-Centrists opposed the anticlerical program not because they were sympathetic to the Catholic cause, but because the program went against the liberal tradition which they wanted the Republic to respect. Jules Simon, an agnostic, opposed the laicization of the primary schools because it was illiberal and because he regarded it as a policy of *revanche* against the Church. When the government decided in 1886 to replace with Republicans all teachers who were priests, Simon opposed it as a violation of the concept of equal rights. The decision to replace clerical teachers, he argued, should be left to the communes, where individual rights could be more easily safeguarded. He hastened to add that if these decisions were made on the local level, he would vote against the Church.[33]

This group of Liberals declined in influence as the decade of the 1880's progressed. Most of its members were past their prime. They were more familiar with the political ideals of the mid-century and seemed unable to understand the politics of a

---

[32] Daniel, *L'Année politique,* pp. 194–196.
[33] Evelyn M. Acomb, *The French Laic Laws, 1879–1889* (New York, 1941), p. 179. See also Georges Weill, *Histoire de l'idée laïque en France au XIXe siècle* (Paris, 1929), p. 284.

younger generation of Republicans. After 1885 the Left-Centrists were excluded from the ruling circles of the Republic.

At the other extreme of the Republican majority were the Radicals. This loosely organized group, which lumped the moderate Henri Brisson with the ferocious Clemenceau, considered itself to be the spiritual heir of the Jacobin tradition and therefore the guardian of the true Republican ideal. The true Republic, according to the Radicals, should be governed by one chamber depending directly upon universal suffrage. Here was reflected the Jacobin faith in the Convention of the Great Revolution. It should have a tax structure which would not favor the moneyed classes, and for that reason the Radicals came to support the progressive income tax. Finally, the true Republic should be completely divorced from any and all religious institutions. The only way that this could be achieved was through the separation of church and state.

Between 1877 and 1885 this group was not particularly strong in the Chamber, but unlike the Left-Center it had grass-roots support. This was revealed in the elections of 1885. During the campaign the Radicals stressed the futility of colonialist ventures which turned the attention of the nation away from the thin blue line of the Vosges. Although the results of the election indicated that the majority of voters was not in favor of great economic or constitutional reform or the separation of church and state, it did show that the electorate was sympathetic to the Radical appeal to patriotic sentiments. The Radicals were able to defeat Opportunist candidates in a number of departments,[34] and, having increased their number in the Chamber, they forced the Opportunists, who until 1885 had governed by themselves, to include them in their various ministries. Thus 1885 was a crucial year in the development of the political structure of the Third Republic, for it was in this year that the "concentration" ministries first came into being. This type of ministry included

[34] Daniel, *L'Année politique,* p. 227.

all elements of the Republican majority with the exception of the Left-Center, but it could be effective only when and if these elements agreed on fundamental issues. From the beginning it was apparent that "concentration" was not the answer to the increasing number of social and economic problems which confronted France at the time. Any ministry which attempted to move forcefully in these areas soon found itself abandoned by a significant element which had supported it. Thus if the Radicals could not achieve their ideal Republic on their own, they could at least prevent the Opportunists from undoing what had already been done, or from compromising Republican principles. They did this by appealing continually to Republican orthodoxy. This technique, which always embarrassed the Opportunists, was to be particularly effective during the period of the *Ralliement*.[35]

The Opportunists, the largest group in the Republican majority, constituted an amorphous political unit whose politics for that reason is particularly hard to define. They were the followers of Gambetta and Jules Ferry, who, in the period between 1881 and 1885, were frequently at odds—especially on questions of colonial policy. They dominated the Chamber from 1876 to 1902, but because they were unable to agree precisely on a number of key issues, they could never completely control the situation despite their numerical superiority.

The political scientist, François Goguel, has stated that from 1881 on, the Opportunists were separated from the Conservatives only on the constitutional question and the religious issue.[36] This was true of the Left-Centrists and of some Opportunists like Jules Méline, the leader of the Protectionist movement so popular among Conservatives. But since the Right and the Left-Centrists violently criticized the public works projects and the

---

[35] For the best analysis of Radical politics to date see Jacques Kayser, *Les grandes batailles du radicalisme* (Paris, 1962).

[36] Goguel, *La politique des partis*, p. 55.

spending policy of the various Opportunist ministries between 1881 and 1885, it is difficult to see how Goguel's thesis can be entirely substantiated. The Opportunists were less interested in reform than the Radicals, but some of their cherished projects such as the free and compulsory primary school were costly. For this reason the Opportunists were committed to a policy of spending which was incompatible with the financial principles of the Right.

On the constitutional question the Opportunists accepted the *status quo*. They approved of the institutions prescribed by the laws of 1875 and therefore defended parliamentary government as it then existed. Few Opportunists supported Boulanger in his quest for revision. According to the followers of Gambetta and Ferry, it was not the institutions which caused ministerial instability, but the factiousness of political groups within them. They believed that the demands of Conservatives and Radicals for constitutional change were detrimental to parliamentary government.

Although it has been suggested that the Opportunists adopted an anticlerical program in order to destroy the Right[37] or because it partially satisfied the clamor from the left,[38] it is unfair to accuse men like Jules Ferry and Eugène Spuller of having sponsored an entirely negative policy toward the Church. Certainly they disliked its close association with the Monarchists and Bonapartists, but there was more to the anticlerical policy of the Opportunists than that. Like the Radicals, they believed that the Church had too much influence in the country; and they were convinced that they could limit this influence by secularizing primary education. This was done in 1882. It was also under their auspices that the principle by which clerical teachers were to be replaced gradually by lay teachers in State primary schools was adopted in 1886. The Opportunists supported a law

[37] Dansette, *Le Boulangisme*, p. 3.
[38] Acomb, *The French Laic Laws*, p. 81.

permitting divorce in 1884 and the *loi militaire* of 1887, which made seminarists available for military service (*curés-sac-au-dos*), because these laws were compatible with the principles of democracy.[39]

The Opportunists did differ from the Radicals on the question of the separation of church and state. The Radicals felt that separation was essential to the welfare of the state. The Opportunists saw it as possibly enhancing the power of the Church. By maintaining the Concordat the government could control and, where necessary, combat religious influence. Paul Cambon, the great diplomat who was closely associated with the Opportunists, brought this out in a letter to his wife written on November 3, 1881.

The Concordat is a treaty designed to limit the authority . . . of the Church. This treaty is essential since the Church obeys a foreign power which can only be dealt with by such a treaty . . . It is true that the Church accepts only those clauses of the Concordat which are to her advantage and balks at those which are not. It is up to the state to prevent such balking and it is prepared for that. It would be a mistake to give the Church the freedom it wants in a country where the vast majority are Catholic and therefore subject, to some extent, to a foreign power . . .

The day when freedom is given to religious organizations as well as the right for the Church to participate in public instruction the country would be swallowed up by the Church within fifty years.[40]

By 1890 the Opportunists had established the principle of secular education, re-established divorce, and abolished clerical exemptions from the army; in short, they had gone about as far as they intended in pushing the claims of the Republic against those of the Church. Because they believed that the Catholics made up a substantial element of public opinion, they were anxious not to push too far. They felt that much could be gained

[39] Jules Dietz, "Jules Ferry et les traditions républicaines," *Revue Politique et Parlementaire*, 161:138–141 (October 10, 1934).

[40] Henri Cambon, ed., *Correspondance de Paul Cambon 1870–1924* (Paris, 1940), I, 139–140. See also Acomb, *The French Laic Laws*, pp. 35–37.

by making the French clergy lay down its arms and accept the Opportunist Republic. Although the Opportunists insisted upon destroying clerical influence in certain areas throughout the 1880's, they also tried to be conciliatory wherever possible. As President Grévy wrote to Leo XIII in 1883:

. . . thanks to Parliament's disposition, animated by moderate and conciliatory sentiments, we can look forward to better times. If Your Holiness perseveres in his attitude, which is the reflexion of his benevolence and great understanding of present conditions, and which meets with the respectful approval of all enlightened friends of religion and public order, and if the hostile element of the clergy disarms, we can look forward to an end to these regrettable quarrels and an enduring pacification of political tempers in the near future.[41]

This desire for pacification reflects the true conservatism of the Opportunists. Having established the Republic and having successfully defended it against the Monarchists and the Church, they soon saw that their next problem was to defend the *status quo* from the attacks of the Left, which grew increasingly strong after 1885. Unfortunately the "concentration" ministries, which became the established form of government after 1885, made it very difficult to achieve appeasement. Rouvier's ministry of 1887 revealed this problem. For despite Rouvier's desire to reach some sort of agreement with the Right, he could not remain in power unless he placated the Radicals, and it was under this ministry that the *loi militaire* was passed in the Chamber.[42]

To many moderate Republicans it seemed sensible to try to convince the Right of the efficacy of Opportunist politics and to make the Conservatives realize that true conservatism was represented by the Opportunists. The need for such a shift in tactics was greater because of Conservative gains in the elections of 1885. In that year Paul Cambon wrote to his wife:

The real losers were the moderate Republicans, that is to say ourselves. The defeat hurts our influence, but we must not give up hope

[41] T'serclaes, *Le Pape Léon XIII*, I, 308.
[42] Goguel, *La politique des partis*, p. 62.

because of this defeat. To people of good sense it is obvious that the Republic is looked upon with horror because it is too sectarian and too violent, and that Monarchy has no roots in the country, and that the Monarchists are too divided, and that after a time of trouble [he seems to anticipate the Boulanger crisis] it will be necessary to return to a sort of Bordeaux Pact as in the time of M. Thiers. It will be up to the moderate Republicans to achieve this.[43]

In a speech to the departmental council of the Vosges quoted in *La Droite Républicaine* (December 26, 1886), Jules Ferry emphasized the need for Monarchists and Bonapartists to become true conservatives.

It does the country no good when part of its strength is consumed in impotent protest. A well-constituted Republic must have a conservative party. It is a noble desire to want to temper a democracy, to sober it, to contain it, but to fulfill this desire one must not separate oneself from the Republic.

Although this desire to conciliate the Right was strong on the part of the Opportunists, it would not be achieved by compromising any Republican principles or by modifying any "Republican" legislation. The Conservatives would have to accept the Republic on Republican terms. As Freycinet said in 1885, it might be desirable to create a two-party system (Whig-Tory), but it would have to be strictly within the Republican framework.[44]

The Opportunists went into the elections of 1889 *en bloc* with the Radicals. In order to combat the rising tide of Boulangism, Republican unity was essential. They emerged from these elections stronger than they had been in 1885. The Tirard-Constans ministry, which consisted mostly of Opportunists, resumed the policy of appeasement which had been abandoned on the eve of the Boulanger crisis. Constans indicated to De Mackau, head of the *Union des droites,* that the government would be conciliatory wherever possible,[45] and it was lenient in its policy of

[43] Cambon, *Correspondance de Paul Cambon,* I, 255.
[44] Maxime Lecomte, *Les Ralliés. Histoire d'un parti 1886–98* (Paris, 1899), pp. 56–57.
[45] Dansette, *Le Boulangisme,* p. 380.

suspending the salaries of those priests who had involved themselves in the electoral campaign.[46] At the same time Spuller, the foreign minister, indicated to the Vatican that the Republic was anxious to put an end to clerical hostility.[47]

4

The Boulanger crisis ended in 1889 with the flight of the General and victory for the Republicans in the elections of that year. The Vatican was more than ever convinced of the need to come to terms with the Republic because of the compromised position of the French Church and the Conservatives. As long as France suffered from internal disorders, she could never be counted on as an effective instrument of Vatican policy. At the same time, many Conservatives realized that they had seriously weakened their political effectiveness because of their role in the Boulanger affair. The Right had lost approximately forty-seven seats in the elections of 1889, and the question of how best to defend conservative principles without sacrificing unity was again raised.[48]

The stage was set for the *Ralliement*. The Vatican and the French government had indicated a general desire for appeasement. Would the Right and the French Church renounce their attitude of hostility toward the Republic? De Mackau had indicated that the *Union des droites* could be conciliatory when he sought to negotiate with Ernest Constans. It remained to be seen whether the Vatican, the French Church, the Conservatives, and the Opportunists could coordinate their respective interests in a way which would be beneficial to all.

[46] Daniel, *L'Année politique*, p. 230.
[47] *Le Figaro*, March 9, 1890.
[48] Seignobos, *L'Évolution de la Troisième République*, p. 147.

CHAPTER II
The Ralliement
1 8 9 0 - 1 8 9 3

On the morrow of the Boulanger crisis adherents of the French Right found themselves in a position similar to that of 1881, when Bonapartists and Monarchists saw their hopes shattered by Republican victories at the polls. Some, such as Paul de Cassagnac, refused to admit that the very existence of the Conservatives was being threatened. Said De Cassagnac in *L'Autorité* of May 24, 1890:

When our discouraged friends pathetically enumerate the battles which they have waged and lost, they seem to forget the three million five hundred thousand votes which supported them and that this number of opposition votes—opposing not only the direction but the form of government—has never been reached in France or in any other country . . .

But at least one observer indicated how badly shaken Conservative opinion really was when he wrote, "How can one help but be affected by such things as the rapid disintegration of the Conservative party, which for lack of direction continues to crumble away?" [1] Another indication of this desperate situation was the appearance in France of the exiled Duc d'Orléans, son and heir of the Comte de Paris, to fulfill his military obligations. Knowing that he would be arrested as soon as he arrived on French soil, it seemed obvious that both he and his father wished to revive the flagging spirits of his supporters with this patriotic gesture.

On January 24, 1890, sixty Conservative deputies gathered together under the presidency of the Comte de Maillé. Bishop

---

[1] H. Delorme, "Le chronique politique," *Le Correspondant*, 123:214 (April 10, 1890).

Freppel, deputy from Finistère and passionately devoted to the Royalist cause, repeated the argument that the Right must maintain unity on the grounds of economic conservatism. This group which continued to call itself the *Union des droites* elected the Duc de Doudeauville, the Baron de Mackau, and Jacques Piou as officers. No new ideas were presented at this meeting, nothing to indicate that the Conservatives were prepared to adopt a new approach to the political situation.[2]

On May 24, 1890, the Duc de Broglie, former premier and Thiers' adversary in the formative years of the Third Republic, attempted to define a possible policy for the Right in a speech before the *Association de la presse monarchique et catholique*. First he took up the question of accepting the form of the Republic:

Because the Republican party has survived the recent shock [of the Boulanger crisis], some of us have asked if the time has not come to proclaim a truce on the question of the constitution in the name of the conservative principles to which we are devoted, and to bring to the Republic not only the submission which is owed to any legal authority, but a formal and sincere adherence, thereby relegating the possibility of a restoration, if not to oblivion, at least to the unforseeable future.

He then proceeded to list the sins and omissions of the Republic, ending with the statement that he was and would remain a Royalist. But rather than adopt the Cassagnac approach of unbending hostility to all things Republican, he urged Conservatives to join with Republicans whenever necessary on important issues.

Are there not questions apart from the Constitution upon which most patriotic Frenchmen can agree? Republicans and Monarchists should feel the same about matters pertaining to defense, *grandeur*, finance, freedom of religion, the maintenance of law and order, and justice. Should there be any difficulty in agreeing every day, question by question, on a number of points? We admit privately that only

[2] *La France Nouvelle,* January 25, 1890.

under the Monarchy can the basic interests of the nation be best maintained.

This does not mean, however, that we should constantly oppose the Republicans. We should associate with anyone in order that the basic interests of the nation will not be needlessly compromised under the Republic.

Conservatives should not practice a *politique de pire* by invariably opposing the Republicans. They should be publicly conservative and privately monarchist. De Broglie revealed at the end of his speech how personal and deep-rooted were his monarchist convictions:

> At this point I would go so far as to express a wish which I scarcely dare utter publicly because there is so little chance of its being fulfilled that I fear I will not be taken seriously. It is that by a return to a conservative majority, of which there is certainly no indication, power would be restored to those who, without contesting the principle of the Republic, would reform its practices. I am convinced that after a short experience along these lines, such a majority would recognize that neither the wisdom nor the ability of a worker, nor his best intentions can improve a faulty machine.[3]

De Cassagnac and De Broglie represented two points of view prevalent in right-wing circles. There was a third, inspired no doubt by the failure of Boulangism. It was to this attitude that De Broglie referred when he spoke of those who were willing to make a truce with the Republicans on the constitutional question in order to defend their ideals.

The leading spokesman for this point of view was Jacques Piou, a deputy from the Haute-Garonne since 1885. The son of a Liberal deputy to the National Assembly of 1871, Piou had made a name for himself as a provincial lawyer in Toulouse. Elected to the Chamber as a Monarchist in 1885, he was disillusioned even then with that cause. Because of his talents and his power as an orator, Jacques Piou quickly became a leading figure in the *Union des droites*. He was a member of the Committee of Twelve which

[3] *La France Nouvelle*, May 25, 1890.

directed right-wing activities for Boulanger, and in 1890 he was elected one of the presidents of the *Union des droites*.[4]

On November 13, 1889, shortly after the elections of that year, *Le Soleil,* an Orleanist paper, published an interview with Piou. Said the deputy from the Haute-Garonne:

> What have we seen for the last fourteen years? Conservatives who have the support of the vast majority in the country a minority in Parliament because the voters fear a leap in the dark and refuse to face the possibility of a crisis the outcome of which they cannot foresee.

Conservatives, he continued, would have to accept the fact of the Republic, and their opposition would have to reflect that acceptance. However, this did not imply adherence to the Republic. It meant only that Conservatives should act in terms of the present situation. Piou agreed with the general Conservative view that religious and financial questions demanded immediate attention and that the laic laws had to be modified substantially.

At this point Piou was reluctant to form a parliamentary group.

> I have neither the inclination nor the time to form a group. Besides I oppose the system of groups, and I would rather not divide the Right. The Right should remain unified, compact and resolute in the defense of tolerance, justice and liberty.

Asked whether he was a "républicain résigné," he replied, "I am simply a man of good will and of good faith who does not shy away from the inevitable." Piou's commitment to the principle of Conservative unity was clearly indicated not only in the interview with *Le Soleil* but also by his acceptance of his election as an officer of the *Union des droites* two months later; it helps to explain his rather hesitant approach to politics between 1890 and 1893.

Despite Piou's distaste for forming parliamentary groups, his objections were somehow overcome. On March 21, 1890, Gaston

[4] Joseph Denais, *Un apôtre de la liberté, Jacques Piou* (Paris, 1959), chap. 1. See also Félix Ribeyre, *La Nouvelle chambre 1885–89* (Paris, 1886), pp. 361–362.

Calmette published an account in *Le Figaro* of a meeting of a group which called itself *La Droite constitutionnelle* and whose leader was Jacques Piou. An unidentified spokesman for this group insisted that it was a part of the Right and that it intended to remain so. He went on to say:

What we want is to draw up a platform for the next general election [1893]: to show the country that there is a constitutional opposition composed of sober Conservatives, statesmen who could conceivably become men of government under the Republic itself, who would safeguard the interests of everyone, who would reestablish order in the public finances, who would reestablish security in internal and external affairs, thereby saving France from the misfortune of a revolution.

On March 31, the *Droite constitutionnelle* published a program in *Le Figaro* which was in substance similar to that of the *Union des droites* of 1885. The program included the following: recognition of existing institutions, which could only be changed by the electorate freely consulted (a major deviation from the position taken by the *Union des droites*); fiscal responsibility—no loans, no new taxes, and sharp reduction of public spending; abrogation of the law exiling heads of former ruling families; greater authority to local government, particularly on matters of education; re-establishment of religious instruction in those primary schools requesting it; improvement in the *loi militaire* to the extent that seminarians would be exempted from infantry training.

Piou did not wish to revive Raoul-Duval's *Droite républicaine,* which had not been well received by Conservatives. He wanted instead to proceed cautiously without causing any embarrassment to the *Union des droites*. If his group was willing to cooperate with the government when the occasion arose, such an attitude was not very different from that of De Broglie. The Calmette article and the program of March 31 indicated that the relatively conciliatory position of the *Droite constitutionnelle* was motivated by a greater interest in economic and social problems than in the constitutional question.

Le Temps of March 21, 1890 listed sixteen deputies who were members of the new parliamentary group (see appendix A). Of the sixteen, eleven came from departments in the north of France —five from the Nord, two from the Calvados, two from the Seine-et-Oise, one from the Marne, and one from the Aisne. The rest were scattered among the Haute-Garonne, the Cher, and the Aveyron. Seven had presented themselves as Constitutional Revisionists in 1889, two as Liberal Constitutionalists who admitted that the form of government was no longer in question, and the rest as Conservatives. Of the sixteen, only three had been deputies before 1885, and of these three, two had been Bonapartists and one an uncommitted Conservative. The vast majority of the members of this group had no deep commitments either to the Comte de Paris or to Prince Victor Bonaparte. They were for the most part landowners or industrialists and were primarily concerned with economic and social questions. All were protectionists, and it is interesting to note that Desjardins, Des Rotours (who was shortly to join the group), and Le Gavrien were closely associated with the Opportunist leader Jules Méline in the *Association de l'Industrie,* an organization which advocated the adoption of protection.[5]

The northern departments, particularly the Nord and the Pas-de-Calais, were acutely affected by changing economic conditions. The concentration of heavy industry in this area and the development of new agricultural techniques at the end of the nineteenth century had created problems which were bound to influence conservative opinion. This explains why members of the *Droite constitutionnelle* were concerned with economic and social questions, and why northern Conservatives in particular

[5] *Le Figaro,* March 10, 1890. For a discussion of the background of the members of the *Droite constitutionnelle* see David Shapiro, "The Ralliement in the Politics of the 1890's" in David Shapiro, ed., *The Right in France, 1890–1919* (London, 1962), pp. 13–48.

felt the need to establish some sort of *modus vivendi* with the Republic.[6]

Despite the group's efforts to maintain a harmonious relationship with the *Union des droites,* its position *vis-à-vis* both the Right and the Republicans was a difficult one. As De Broglie had pointed out, acceptance of existing institutions meant ultimate adherence to them. The distinction between "acceptance" and "adherence" is important to the understanding of the tactical situation of the *Droite constitutionnelle.* Acceptance of the form of the Republic or of existing institutions by a Conservative did not commit him to support of the Republic in the future if ever there was a strong possibility for a Restoration. Adherence to the Republic committed the Conservatives to a defense of the Republic under any circumstances whatsoever. If De Broglie rejected any possibility of adherence, others such as Francis Magnard, editor of *Le Figaro* and former associate of Raoul-Duval, felt that adherence was essential if Piou and his followers were to succeed (*Le Figaro,* June 2, 1890). An editorial in *Le Petit Moniteur Universel* on November 23, 1890, by Ernest Daudet, brother of Alphonse, indicated that the question of tactics was creating considerable confusion among the members of the new group. "Some members want to move very slowly and prudently toward adherence; others, if they could, would move rapidly in that direction. Some would continue to associate with the *Union des droites,* others would not."

The right wing of the group had an articulate spokesman in Jules Delafosse, deputy from the Calvados, former Bonapartist, and ardent supporter of General Boulanger. In an article published in *Le Matin* on March 25, six days before the publication of the program of the *Droite constitutionnelle,* he indicated that his hostile attitude toward the Republic had not changed.

We are not Republicans because being such implies loyalty to a body of concepts, doctrines and attitudes against which our conscience

[6] Seignobos, *L'Évolution de la IIIe République,* pp. 409–467.

protests. We do not consider, however, that the Republic must be governed by Republicans . . .

We want to take over the Republic and realize through the Republic the good that other reactionaries or visionaries expect from a restoration whose prospects are dim to say the least . . .

We feel that the Republic is imperfect and we reserve the right to demand constitutional revision. We are inclined to be sympathetic to those moderate Republicans who wish to curb the iniquitous effects of the Republic. But we rely only on ourselves for a complete reform, and, the country being willing, we shall succeed . . .

France is worth more than the unworthy and brutal regime to which she has submitted, and France the liberator shall deliver herself from it as she has from so many others. I sense in the present political situation that this liberation is imminent.

Delafosse was still under the influence of Boulangism. His attitude toward the Republic was aggressive and hostile, while at the same time scornful of those Conservatives who would not join the *Droite constitutionnelle*. In terms of political realities, what did this sort of independence signify? If Republicans and Intransigent Conservatives were hostile, how could a small parliamentary group hope to be effective? Delafosse implied that the *Droite constitutionnelle* had the tacit support of the majority of French voters. Despite his attempts to define clearly his concept of political independence, it is difficult to see exactly what his acceptance of that "unworthy and brutal regime," the Republic, involved.

For the left wing of the new group the problem of accepting the Republic was less difficult.

. . . the hour has come for Conservatives to enter the Republic, not as an act of abdication but as a way of creating a constitutional terrain which would work to bring about a majority in Parliament and in the country.

So wrote Daudet in *Le Petit Moniteur Universel* on April 3, 1890. He wanted the group to take up the position established by the *Droite républicaine* in 1886. At that time the idea of creating a "Tory" party within the framework of the Republic had not appealed to the Right as a whole. The danger of the left-wing approach was that it might incur the same hostility.

The formation of the *Droite constitutionnelle* was followed closely by both the Right and the Opportunists. To the Right it offered a course of action in a time of need, and to the Opportunists it indicated that Conservatives might lay down their arms and accept the existing institutions. But even in that year it was clear that Piou's group would not be able to induce the *Union des droites* to adopt its approach. In his editorials, De Cassagnac insisted that the hostile and aggressive policy of the Right in the 1880's was still feasible for the 1890's. De Broglie and his followers were willing to be conciliatory and even to cooperate with the moderate Republicans, but for them the *Droite constitutionnelle* went beyond acceptable limits in its relationship with the Republic as stated in its manifesto of March 31. The Marquis de Ville-bois-Marteuil, a Royalist, defined the limits in *La France Nouvelle* on October 24, 1890 as follows:

Royalists, powerless to bring about a government of their choice, will adopt a role of absolute neutrality and will concern themselves with the questions of the day. In order to do this they feel that it is unnecessary to issue declarations, manifestos, or to form a group.

For Piou and his followers the question of limits was equally difficult, and for this reason their political position in 1890 was enigmatic. "Are the members of the *Droite constitutionnelle* Republicans without saying it, or are they saying that they are Republicans without being Republicans?" asked the editors of the conservative *La France Nouvelle* (October 24, 1890). As the year progressed, it became obvious that until the group could definitely decide in which direction it should move, it would have very little influence on either the Right or the Republicans. As Francis Magnard wrote in *Le Figaro* on September 11, 1890, "Our poor *Droite constitutionnelle* has not cut a very good figure in the last six months . . ."

2

On November 12, 1890, at a dinner given in honor of a French squadron which had put in at Algiers, the host, Cardinal Lavigerie, Primate of North Africa, raised his glass in a toast to the French navy. After greeting the guests in the name of the Governor-General, who was absent, the Cardinal touched upon the subject of unity.

In view of a difficult past and menacing future, we have at this moment a great need for unity. Harmonious relations among all good citizens, need I say, is the cherished wish of the Church.

Certainly the Church does not expect us to surrender our memories of the past, nor those sentiments of fidelity which are honorable in all men. But when the will of a people has made itself clear as to a form of government which conforms to those principles which alone can preserve Christian nations according to the encyclicals of Leo XIII, *when adherence without reservations* to that form of government can save that nation from the abyss which yawns before it, then the moment has come to sacrifice all that honor and conscience permit for the safety of our country in order to put an end to our divisions.

This is what I have taught, this is the attitude which I would like to see our clergy in France adopt, and in saying this I am certain that I will not be contradicted by any ecclesiastical authority.

Other than this resignation, this patriotic acceptance, there is no other way to save the world from the menace of socialism, or to save that faith of which we are the ministers.[7]

The reaction of the audience was frigid. Admiral Duperre had to be prompted by the Cardinal before he replied, "I drink to his Eminence the Cardinal and to the clergy of Algeria," whereupon the band of the College of St. Eugène struck up *"La Marseillaise"* at Lavigerie's instigation.[8]

Many Catholics and Conservatives tried to believe that Cardinal Lavigerie was expressing his own opinion and that the appeal

---

[7] Quoted in Tournier, *Le Cardinal Lavigerie* (Paris, 1913), pp. 287–288. Italics are mine.

[8] *Ibid.*, p. 289.

for adherence to the Republic was not inspired by the Vatican. The Cardinal had been in Rome, however, in October of 1890, and he had suggested to Leo XIII that the internal divisions in France could be healed if a high ecclesiastical figure would publicly advocate formal adherence to the Republic. The Pope had agreed in principle, although he indicated that he did not want to be directly associated with such a statement since it would look as though he were interfering in internal politics.[9] Further indication that the Vatican supported Cardinal Lavigerie's position came in a letter written by Cardinal Rampolla, Vatican Secretary of State, to the Bishop of St.-Flour on December 9, 1890. Rampolla stressed the point made by Leo XIII in his encyclical *Immortale Dei* to the effect that the Church had no special preference for any form of government as long as that government conformed to natural law. He then went on to say:

Consequently, when the interests of religion demand it, and there is no just reason to oppose it, it is right that the faithful participate in public affairs in order that through their zeal and their authority, existing institutions and laws will be modelled on the rules of justice, and that the spirit and salutary effect of religion will influence the general welfare of the state.

Now as regards the Catholics of France, there is no doubt that they would be performing a useful and salutary work if, considering the state that their country has been in for some time, they follow the path which will lead them quickly and efficaciously toward the goal which I have indicated.[10]

Cardinal Lavigerie's toast and Cardinal Rampolla's letter reflected the Vatican concerns discussed in the preceding chapter. There was the appeal for unity, which echoed Leo XIII's *Nobilissima Gallorum gens;* there was the same concern for the condition of the French Church; and finally, there was the same insistence upon the need to maintain order and authority in the

---

[9] Louis Baunard, *Léon XIII et le toast d'Alger: Souvenirs et documents de deux audiences pontificales intimes le 24 et le 26 avril 1896* (Paris, 1914), pp. 25–33.
[10] Quoted in Tournier, *Le Cardinal Lavigerie,* pp. 302–303.

face of the socialist menace. Here Lavigerie and Rampolla echoed not only the utterances of the Pope, but also the *Droite constitutionnelle's Declaration* of March 31, 1890. Lavigerie had been in Paris in September 1890, and had had long discussions with President Carnot and Premier Freycinet. He was therefore *au courant* with the political situation in France. There can be no question but that the toast at Algiers was carefully timed to coincide with shifting developments on the French political scene.[11]

The reaction of the French clergy to the toast was lukewarm but on the whole affirmative. The attitude of the bishops had always been one of respect toward the civil authority of the Third Republic, and they opposed it only when religious interests were menaced. As Bishop Turinaz of Nancy, who had always been a vociferous opponent of the laic legislation, said, ". . . we have never indicated any hostility toward the form of the Republic . . ." [12] Even Bishop Isoard of Annecy, one of France's more reactionary clerics, accepted the basic ideas expressed by Cardinal Lavigerie.[13]

In terms of political action French Catholics, lay and clerical, reacted to the toast in three ways. Bishop Fava of Grenoble declared that he would adhere loyally to the Republic. He advocated the formation of a Catholic party which would devote its energies to doing battle with the Republicans for the Republic. Like so many French clerics he made the distinction between form and substance. The Republic which he was willing to accept was not the Republic as it stood, but a Republic whose policies would be determined by the Church. This approach neatly avoided the dilemma which confronted the *Droite constitutionnelle,* and it was popular with the clergy.[14]

An even more popular political reaction to the toast among Catholics and Conservatives alike was the *Union de la France*

[11] Dansette, *Histoire religieuse de la France contemporaine,* II, 129.
[12] *L'Observateur Français,* January 6, 1891.
[13] Tournier, *Le Cardinal Lavigerie,* p. 292.
[14] *L'Éclair,* July 4, 1891 and *Le Figaro,* July 6, 1891.

chrétienne inspired by Cardinal Richard, Archbishop of Paris. On June 22, 1891, this group published the following declaration:

French Catholics! We are not forming another party, which would only add to the political divisions of France. We represent Christian France, debased, humiliated, and persecuted. We are preparing for the defense of its rights and the vindication of its liberties.

We undertake this defense by all legal means which are available to us, by the press, by the spoken word, by petition and by the ballot.

The program which we present is nothing more than the reflection of those sentiments which stir the hearts of all Catholics. We will stand by this program as long as Christian France has to recover its rights and its liberties at the hands of her children through the grace of God.

Ready for action, Catholics of France, we march to battle, hand in hand. God will fight with us because He is always on the side of those who, without thinking of themselves, work to establish His kingdom on earth and struggle for their faith, the honor of their family, for the Christian education of their children, for their Church and for their country.

The main points of the program of the *Union de la France chrétienne* were: freedom for the Church, for religious orders, and for hospitals; no work on Sundays; revision of the *loi scolaire* where it conflicted with religious interests and family rights; reform of the *loi militaire;* re-establishment of chaplains in the army and navy in peace and war; legislation for better working conditions; and the election of Christian candidates.[15]

The *Union de la France chrétienne* made no mention of the constitution. It considered itself above politics and relied upon a purely religious program which it hoped would appeal to all Conservatives. Like the *Union des droites,* it felt that no mention of the constitutional question was in itself an adequate admission that the Republic existed. The Richard group and the Fava group differed on the problem of adherence, but their approach was essentially the same. Both interpreted the toast and Cardinal

[15] Program of the *Union de la France chrétienne,* A. N. F19 5612.

Rampolla's letter to the Bishop of St.-Flour as a call to arms against the policies of the Third Republic.

Jules Bonjean's *Association catholique française* represented a third reaction among French Catholics to Cardinal Lavigerie's toast. Bonjean felt that Fava's *Parti catholique* and the *Union de la France chrétienne* were too clerical in their approach to politics. He accepted the Republic and refused to take a rigid line. "The idea of turning Catholicism into a political party runs contrary to the tenets of that faith," he wrote.[16] The *Association catholique française* emphasized the need for appeasement, and here it differed fundamentally with the other two organizations. But if Bonjean's movement was received enthusiastically by the Opportunist press and by left-wing elements of the *Droite constitutionnelle*, it was unable to convince most French Catholics that appeasement was more advantageous than an aggressive and hostile policy.[17] For them the laic laws remained the key issue. Would a policy of appeasement bring about a revision of the *loi scolaire* and the *loi militaire*? If Catholics were to accept the Republic, would they not have to make it clear that they were still violently opposed to this legislation? This problem, which was ultimately to affect the course of the *Ralliement*, was clearly stated in a letter to the editor of *Le Correspondant*, a Catholic review.

It would be deplorable if adherence to the Republic involved the abandonment of all the legitimate grievances and well-founded complaints which we have always voiced.[18]

The attitude of intransigent Conservatives toward Cardinal Lavigerie's toast was best illustrated by the frigid silence with which the officers of the Mediterranean squadron received it. For them the problem of distinguishing between Republican

---

[16] Jules Bonjean, "Le Mouvement catholique et la politique générale," *Nouvelle Revue*, 72:673 (October 15, 1891).

[17] In addition to Bonjean's article see Ernest Daudet's editorial in *L'Exprèss de Lyon*, February 10, 1891; *Le Figaro*, September 4, 1891; Dansette, *Histoire religieuse de la France contemporaine*, II, 135.

[18] *Le Correspondant*, 127:5 (April 10, 1890).

form and substance did not exist; they were one and the same. Accepting the Republic meant bowing to the will of Republican legislators. The most comprehensive statement of the Intransigent position after the toast was a speech given in Nîmes on February 8, 1891, by the Comte d'Haussonville, the Comte de Paris' representative in France (quoted in *Le Figaro* on the following day). D'Haussonville was responding both to the toast and to the formation of the *Droite constitutionnelle* when he pointed out that Lavigerie had a perfect right to offer his opinion, but that it was only an opinion; that if the Church made no distinction between types of constitutions, it could not prefer one to another. The implication here was that the Vatican was meddling in internal affairs. The Count referred to Lavigerie's insistence that in any political action an individual must be guided by his honor and by his conscience. It was precisely this that the Monarchists were doing when they advocated their cause over that of the Republic. Honor could not permit the renunciation of a cause which was sacred.

Nor could our conscience permit us to adhere to the Republic after having denounced it as intolerant, after having reproached it for wounding conscience and troubling religious peace in chasing God from schools and hospitals. Rightly or wrongly we remain persuaded that the Republic is somehow riveted by chains bound to the past and to this policy of intolerance. Those who are today at its head, and those who aspire to be, give us no hope that there will be a let-up in the application of those laws which we have denounced as detestable. Each day that passes convinces us more that this is so. Never is the weak and fluctuating majority which supports this policy more inspired than when it hears the old battle-cry, "Clericalism, that is to say Christianity, there is the enemy."

The Count hastened to add that Jacques Piou's approach would do nothing to alter the anticlerical sentiments with which the government was imbued. He predicted (correctly) that the Republicans would demand proof of the sincerity of the *Droite constitutionnelle* and that this would entail nothing less than acceptance of the laic laws. D'Haussonville refused to admit that the Right should take the first step in bringing about a general relaxation of political tensions. His basic criticism of Piou and Lavigerie was that they, as the injured party, were taking the first step and that this was tantamount to capitulation. He labeled the policy of the *Ralliement* a policy of abdication.

Although they categorically refused to accept the Republic, the Intransigents were for the most part willing to maintain the neutral position which the *Union des droites* had adopted in 1885. They admitted that for the time being the constitutional question was not an issue, and they had no difficulty accepting the position taken by the *Union de la France chrétienne*. De Mackau, D'Haussonville, De Breteuil, and De Mun, leaders of the *Union des droites,* were sponsors of the new Union, and local electoral committees which supported candidates of the *Union des droites* were placed at the disposal of the *Union de la France chrétienne*.[19] But the cherished if futile belief in a future restoration which had undermined Raoul-Duval's political position in 1886 now prevented a majority of the Conservatives from accepting the ideas of Cardinal Lavigerie.

. . . we are among those who believe that France is monarchist in temperament and that sooner or later—this is the secret of Providence—she will return to those traditions the violation and abandonment of which are the cause of our present woes.[20]

Cardinal Lavigerie's toast and Cardinal Rampolla's letter did provide considerable support for the flagging *Droite constitutionnelle*. Piou was summoned to Rome in February 1891, a further indication that the Vatican supported his position, and the group gained additional members and greater confidence in its ability to affect French politics (*L'Observateur Français,* February 25, 1891). Yet its members were still divided on the question of whether they should move closer to the Republic or remain in association with the other elements of the *Union des droites*.

Thellier de Poncheville, deputy from the Nord, was one of the

---

[19] Dansette, *Histoire religieuse de la France contemporaine,* II, 134–135.
[20] Henri Rémy de Simony, *La République ouverte* (Paris, 1891), p. 17.

chief spokesmen for the right wing of the Piou group. In an article which appeared in *La France Nouvelle* on February 12, 1891, he emphasized the need for Conservative unity, but at the expense of sacrificing the constitutional question forever, if necessary.

I wish that they [the Conservatives] would hold their heads high and fight on ground which they may not have chosen but which events have forced on them.

Conservatives . . . must never stop fighting the sect which is now in power.

Thellier de Poncheville refused to consider cooperation with moderate Republicans, who were too easily swayed by the Radicals. He and his associates deplored the divisions which were weakening the effectiveness of the Right, and in an article in *La France Nouvelle* on February 16, 1891 De Montéty, deputy from the Aveyron, insisted that there was no difference between the members of the *Droite constitutionnelle* and the followers of D'Haussonville.

The left wing of the *Droite constitutionnelle* continued to advocate adherence to the Republic of the Republicans. Daudet, chief spokesman for this element, saw a profound difference between D'Haussonville and the Piou group. He felt that the latter was on the verge of adherence to the Republic. Whereas Thellier de Poncheville and others believed that the success of the group depended upon its ability to persuade Intransigent Conservatives that its political approach would benefit the Right as a whole, Ernest Daudet emphasized the relationship between the *Droite constitutionnelle* and the Opportunists. "The future, as far as I can see, lies with the moderate groups," wrote Hély d'Oissel, another member of the left wing, in *L'Éclair* on February 17, 1891. He added:

The support the moderates will have lost from the Radicals they will find among the Conservatives. This union alone will be fruitful, this union alone can assure a successful defense of conservative principles and the passage of laws which the country awaits.

Before the end of this legislature a great party will be formed consisting of members of the clergy, moderate Republicans, Conservatives of good faith and sincere patriots because of the pressure of events.

Ernest Daudet revealed in *La France Nouvelle* of November 4, 1891 that many of the Opportunists wanted to shake off the yoke of "concentration." "Two members of the present ministry [the fourth Freycinet ministry]—I speak the truth—have said many times to Conservative deputies and journalists, 'Bring us a hundred votes and we will break with the Radicals.'"

This conviction that the *Droite constitutionnelle* should join with the Opportunists was strengthened by the enthusiastic reception of the French fleet at Kronstadt in July 1891. If the Tsar could bring himself to stand bareheaded during a Russian rendition of "*La Marseillaise*," eight months after Cardinal Lavigerie had had it played in Algeria, he must have reached the conclusion that the Republic was firmly entrenched. There was now a definite possibility that France would emerge from her isolation, and Kronstadt represented a diplomatic triumph for the Third Republic. This was difficult to ignore, and some members of the Piou group went so far as to suggest that the warm reception at the Russian naval base resulted from their own acceptance of the Republic and Cardinal Lavigerie's toast. With this in mind, *La Liberté des Hautes-Pyrénées,* a provincial newspaper which supported the *Droite constitutionnelle,* made the following appeal to the government on August 30, 1891:

Act in such a way as to make it unnecessary for us to apologize every time we support you.
. . . Let us help you to attain peace on two fronts, each closely associated with the other. You are aware that you have had the good fortune to see France's supremacy newly assured and that we were involved in the events leading to its re-establishment. Will you deny that it is because it was clear that we were united on the domestic front that you were able to find allies?

At any rate, some of the left-wing members including Hély

d'Oissel, De Montsaulnin, Muller, and Loreau began to vote frequently with the government. It is interesting to note that these
members of the Piou group were younger than the others and
therefore less influenced by political traditions.[21]

As leader of the *Droite constitutionnelle,* Jacques Piou was in
a difficult position. There was considerable difference of opinion
within the group on the question of a precise relationship to the
Republic. He was under pressure from Republicans, Conservatives, and the Church to define that relationship. On February
11, 1891, there appeared in *Le Figaro* an open letter from Piou,
who had just returned from his visit to the Vatican, to the Comte
d'Haussonville, the Comte de Paris' representative in France. In
the letter Piou stated that he had no intention of joining forces
with the Opportunists. "They have their program and we have
ours." He reiterated the point that he had made in the *Soleil*
interview of November 1889 that it was futile to base opposition
to the government entirely upon the constitutional question, and
he insisted, quite correctly, that this had been the conclusion of
most Conservatives since 1885. Piou was saying in effect that he
was not deviating from the traditional policy of the *Union des
droites.* The letter ended on a hostile note with regard to Republicans:

I hear it said, "The Republicans will not open the door to us."
I never asked them to. The keys of the house are not in their hands
but in the hands of the people, and it is from them that we intend to
receive them. We have no concessions to make or conditions to dictate.
We have only to struggle on and merit victory through our efforts and
our sagacity.

Despite Cardinal Lavigerie's toast and Piou's trip to Rome, it
was apparent from the letter to D'Haussonville that the leader
of the *Droite constitutionnelle* was not inclined to go as far as
Lavigerie had demanded in adhering without reservations to the
Republic. At this point he was more concerned about unity in

[21] *Le Figaro,* March 9, 1891.

Conservative ranks than he was about the precise relationship to the Republic. If he proclaimed himself loyal to the Republic, he would weaken rather than strengthen the *Union des droites,* and he was undoubtedly aware of previous efforts of Conservatives to find some effective basis for action.

At the end of the year 1891 there occurred an event which did considerable harm to the policy of appeasement. This was the Gouthe-Soulard crisis. On October 2, 1891, during a pilgrimage of the *Jeunesse catholique* in Rome, some members of the group went into the Pantheon and wrote, *"Vive le pape"* in the visitors' register. They were promptly arrested and imprisoned by the Italian authorities. Anxious to avert further deterioration of Franco-Italian relations, the French government acted quickly, and Fallières, the Minister of Public Worship, sent a letter to all French bishops asking them to suspend such pilgrimages. Many bishops felt that the letter was unjust, since it seemed to place responsibility for the incident on them, and Archbishop Gouthe-Soulard of Aix-en-Provence echoed these sentiments in a letter to Fallières.

We do not need your advice now or in the future . . . We know how to conduct ourselves . . . You talk of peace, but your actions reflect hatred and persecution because Freemasonry, eldest daughter of Satan, guides them.[22]

The Bishop was brought to trial despite the efforts of Mgr. Ferrata, the new papal nuncio in Paris, who feared that such a trial might do irreparable damage to the Vatican's French policy.[23] His salary was suspended, he was fined three thousand francs, and was treated like a hero by a great many Catholics. On January 21, 1892, five French cardinals (not including Lavigerie) published a declaration which reflected the attitude of the clergy after the incident. It listed the grievances of the Church against the Republic and pointed out that the clergy had always

[22] Quoted in Dansette, *Histoire religieuse de la France contemporaine,* II, 136.
[23] Ferrata, *Ma Nonciature en France,* p. 116.

respected civil authority except when it conflicted with religious interests. The five cardinals strongly implied that the government would have to take the first step toward appeasement.[24]

The Chamber debated various aspects of the Gouthe-Soulard affair on December 11, 1891, and the Intransigents took full advantage of this opportunity to castigate the Republic and the policy of appeasement. De Cassagnac was in his element ridiculing the conciliatory attitude adopted by Opportunists and members of the *Droite constitutionnelle* after the Boulanger crisis.

This period, it has been said, and I repeat it, was like a honeymoon. You have heard bishops sing the praises of the Republic, although you will not hear much of that now.

There were those who went even further; you have heard a cardinal put past grievances aside and order *"La Marseillaise"* to be played by the band of the Pères-Blancs. Still the honeymoon.

Now, however, the moon is red.

It is so red that we are presently at the point of discussing the separation of Church and State.[25]

Passions had been so stirred up by the crisis that the question of separation was raised not only by the Radicals but by some Intransigents, including De Cassagnac, who said that "many Catholics no longer want the Concordat. They prefer separation to this Concordat which has been so distorted and falsified." [26] The chief spokesmen for the Church in this debate were De Cassagnac, De Provost de Launay, De Mun, Baudry d'Asson, the Comte de Bernis, De Ramel, and De Mackau. All were Monarchists from the west except De Mackau, who at this point was neutral. The members of the *Droite constitutionnelle* kept silent, but there were indications that at least some of Piou's followers were annoyed by the Gouthe-Soulard affair and the passions it

---

[24] Dansette, *Histoire religieuse de la France contemporaine*, II, 137–138.

[25] Journal Officiel (hereinafter cited as J. O.), Chambre, Débats (December 11, 1891), p. 878.

[26] *Ibid.*, p. 878.

aroused. The *Liberté des Hautes Pyrénées* of December 2, 1891 expressed resentment at the attitude of the Archbishop.

The Archbishop of Aix wrote a letter to his superior which you know about. He was fined three thousand francs and considers himself a martyr because of it. That is his business . . . The vanity of the Archbishop has caused considerable embarrassment even among his friends and for the policy of Leo XIII.

As the year 1891 came to an end, it was questionable whether the movement initiated by Piou and Cardinal Lavigerie—the *Ralliement*—would succeed. The clergy on the whole interpreted the toast and Rampolla's letter as a call to arms; the Intransigents saw in the Gouthe-Soulard incident a justification for their own position; and Piou's group, not knowing which course to follow, was not strong enough to exert any decisive influence. Embarrassed by the taunts of the Radicals, who took up the Gouthe-Soulard affair to further the cause of separation of church and state, the Opportunists questioned the conciliatory policy which they had adopted in 1890. At this point there appeared to be few advocates of a policy of internal appeasement in France.

3

On February 16, 1892, Leo XIII published an encyclical addressed to all French Catholics entitled *Au milieu des sollicitudes*.

We believe that it is opportune and even necessary to raise our voice again to exhort not only Catholics but all honest and sensible Frenchmen to rid themselves of the germ of political dissension and to devote their energies to that end. Everyone knows the price involved in pacification. Yet more and more people demand it. We desire it more than anyone because we are the earthly representative of the God of Peace.[27]

The Pope extolled the virtues of the Christian Faith as represented by the Catholic Church. Only the Church, he said, could

[27] Quoted in *L'Observateur Français*, February 21, 1892.

achieve pacification and imbue society with that morality which binds men to God. "To attain that moral condition . . . a great union is necessary. It is essential to put aside those preoccupations which tend to weaken the strength and efficacy of that union."

Catholics had the right to prefer a certain form of government, said Leo XIII, and he emphasized the point made in *Immortale Dei* that the Church had no particular preference for any form of government as long as it respected the law of God. When a government was legally established, however, it was the duty of Catholics to accept it. "Thus when a new government which represents the immutable power of God is established, it is not only possible but imperative to accept it in order that the common good which created that government be maintained."

In the encyclical the Pope made the important distinction between the form of government and its substance. "Under a regime whose form is excellent the legislation can be detestable." This was the crux of the matter. Most Catholics accepted the Republic but refused to accept the laic legislation. The Pope deplored these laws and said that he had raised his voice against them many times. It was the duty of Catholics to oppose this harmful legislation. The encyclical ended with an appeal to maintain the Concordat, which Leo XIII believed was vital to the welfare of France.

One might well ask how this encyclical differed from the Declaration of the Five Cardinals during the Gouthe-Soulard incident, for the encyclical made the distinction between form and substance which had constantly been made by the French clergy. The difference lay in Leo XIII's tone and in his insistence upon the need to adhere to the Republic. Whereas the Declaration sounded hostile, the encyclical was conciliatory. Furthermore, Leo XIII rejected political action on a strictly Catholic basis and called for the cooperation of Catholics with other "wise and sensible Frenchmen." The Declaration and other episcopal utterances were lukewarm on the question of acceptance, but the encyclical clearly stated that the need for social order and national unity imposed it on all Catholics, whatever their private preferences. Although many Catholics chose to ignore the difference in tone betwen the encyclical and the Declaration, it did exist and was amplified in subsequent statements by the Pope.

In a letter written on May 3, 1892 to the French cardinals and published on May 7th in *L'Observateur Français,* Leo XIII stated that his primary concern was the union of all Frenchmen for the good of their country. This could only be achieved if Frenchmen would forget their differences. Only through Catholic and conservative unity could the Church be saved. "One of the means by which this unity is maintained is the acceptance without reservation[28] and with Christian loyalty of civil authority in the form in which it presently exists in France . . . And the reason for this acceptance is that the common good of society places it above all other demands." In a letter to Bishop Fava on June 22, 1892, Leo XIII again expressed his wish to see Catholics cooperate with other conservatives.[29]

The Pope's desire for the appeasement of political passions in France and for the union of all conservatives to defend the traditions of Western civilization was in keeping with his previous statements and actions. It was certainly to his interest to have a politically stable and conservative France which would oppose socialism and defend the rights of the Church. Only a politically unified France could attract Russia as an ally. Thus an aggressive Catholic opposition, even if it accepted the Republican form, could hardly suit Vatican interests. That was why Leo XIII advocated cooperation with other conservatives, by which he clearly meant the Opportunists. It becomes even more obvious that appeasement and conservative unity were keys to Leo XIII's policy toward France when one considers the timing of the encyclical

---

[28] ". . . sans arrière-pensée." The same phrase was used by Cardinal Lavigerie in the toast at Algiers.

[29] Dansette, *Histoire religieuse de la France contemporaine,* II, 143.

Au milieu des sollicitudes. It came right after the Gouthe-Soulard crisis, when Catholics were in a hostile mood toward the Republicans and when the *Droite constitutionnelle* was having difficulty deciding upon a course of action. Still further clarification of Vatican policy came in a telegram dated December 6, 1891 from the French ambassador at the Vatican to the Quai d'Orsay in which Lefebvre de Béhaine described an interview with Cardinal Rampolla on the subject of the Gouthe-Soulard incident.

The Cardinal said that the Vatican was using every means at its disposal to restore calm by prudent advice to the episcopate through the intermediary of the nuncio in Paris as well as through official organs . . . He then discussed various reasons why he considered that it was essential for the Republic to maintain normal relations with the Church.

According to him, the Republic would find it doubly advantageous to do so. First because it would make it easier to bring about an alliance of center groups in Parliament, and secondly because it would facilitate good relations with Russia.[30]

In order to achieve its diplomatic objectives the Vatican needed the support of the Opportunists, whose influence in French politics was still considerable.

Leo XIII's appeal for the relaxation of political tensions was received unenthusiastically by the French clergy. In an editorial in *Le Figaro* on April 26, 1892, Francis Magnard complained that the attitude of the episcopate negated the spirit of the recent encyclical, and he cited a statement of Bishop Turinaz of Nancy:

I wonder if, over the past nineteen centuries, there has ever been a tyranny as odious, hypocritical, dishonorable and absurd imposed upon a clergy and a Catholic country as the one which exists today in France? The French clergy, which has behind it fourteen centuries of independence, dignity, courage, glory and sometimes heroism, cannot bow its head before such indignities.

In the spring of 1893 the Ministry of Public Worship asked the departmental prefects to report on the activities of the clergy and

[30] A. N. F19 1943.

of the Catholic press with regard to the forthcoming elections. Most of the prefectoral reports showed that the bishops and priests accepted the Republic, except in Brittany, where communion was still refused Republican voters. They were, however, campaigning strongly against the laic legislation. An effective means of preparing Catholics for the elections, according to the prefect of Finistère, was the use of catechisms and diocesan weeklies, one of which instructed its readers that "the first question one must ask oneself upon receiving the ballot is whether the candidate is capable of voting laws contrary to the free exercise of religion in France."[31] The Vatican put an end to this by asking ecclesiastical authorities to withdraw troublesome catechisms.[32] At the same time, Leo XIII had put an end to the idea of a *Parti catholique* in his letter of June 22, 1892, to Bishop Fava in which he urged cooperation between Catholics and other conservatives. Yet the clergy did not feel themselves restricted by these limitations. There were other means of influencing the Catholic voter, particularly through the Catholic press.

The two leading Catholic newspapers were *L'Univers,* founded by Louis Veuillot, and *La Croix*. Because it had always been ultramontanist, *L'Univers* accepted the Vatican position, although some of its editors later broke away to form *La Verité,* which was extremely hostile to the Republicans. *La Croix,* the organ of the Assumptionist Fathers, was by far the most influential Catholic newspaper. It paid lip service to the wishes of the Pope but remained hostile to the Republic. Because of its many local editions (there were few departments which did not publish their own supplement to *La Croix*) this paper was able to have a considerable effect on Catholic opinion on the eve of the elections.

There were some exceptions to the dominantly hostile and

[31] Reports of the departmental prefects to the Ministry of Public Worship, A. N. F19 5619.
[32] *L'Observateur Français,* June 5, 1892.

aggressive attitude of the French clergy. Cardinal Lecot, Archbishop of Bordeaux, understood the desire for conciliation voiced in *Au milieu des sollicitudes* and suggested a temporary acceptance of the laic legislation until a more perfect understanding between various conservative groups had been achieved. But in general the bishops and priests accepted the letter and not the spirit of the encyclical.[33]

The papal encyclical did considerable damage to the old Conservative position. Since 1885 the Right had tried to present a united front on certain critical issues, chief among which was the defense of religious rights. The encyclical destroyed any hope for unified Conservative action short of accepting the Republic. Many leaders of the *Union des droites* either rallied or withdrew from the political scene. De Mackau and De Mun rallied in 1892. The Marquis de Breteuil, a prominent Royalist deputy, resigned his seat in deference both to the wishes of the Vatican and to his personal preferences. The *Union de la France chrétienne,* which was nothing more than a cover for the *Union des droites,* was disbanded in May 1892. Those deputies, mostly from the west, who refused to renounce their belief in a restoration found it difficult to justify their position and to adopt a course of action. On April 7, 1892, there was a meeting of a group which called itself *L'Union de la droite libérale* under the presidency of the Marquis d'Aillières, a Breton deputy. The program of the group involved the vindication of

. . . those liberties which have been constantly violated and which the Right has continued to defend over the last fifteen years: freedom of conscience, freedom of the family, freedom of the communes.

It [the group] advocates security and the free exercise of human rights, financial reform, and a government dedicated to the maintenance of peace and unity. It appeals to all Liberals, regardless of background or degree of belief, in order that they may no longer remain a minority but become a majority.[34]

[33] Reports of the departmental prefects, A. N. F19 5619.
[34] Quoted in *L'Univers,* August 12, 1892.

The program was similar to that of the old *Union des droites,* but it attempted to reach beyond the traditional Conservatives to Republicans by emphasizing the liberal nature of their demands. The group was also trying to find common ground with the *Droite constitutionnelle* in a desperate attempt to restore at least a modicum of unity to the Right. The *Ralliés* and liberal Republicans were not interested.

On September 26, 1892, the Comte d'Haussonville delivered a speech at Montauban attempting once again to justify the Intransigent position.[35] He considered the policy of the Vatican an unwarranted interference in internal affairs and insisted that the only true friends of religion were the Monarchists, who alone understood the ancient traditions of France. He said that monarchy was compatible with democracy and that it gave democracy greater stability. In another speech given before the Monarchist and Catholic Press Association on June 18, 1893, D'Haussonville discussed the policy which the Intransigents should adopt for the coming elections.

I do not think that the honor of our party requires us to raise the constitutional question during the coming campaign.

I am so impressed by the need to maintain unity among the Conservatives that I would offer no advice which might be harmful to it.

We will never renounce our right to be Monarchists. Whatever the result of our efforts, these elections represent only a phase for us . . .

In France no one, I repeat, no one, not even among the Republicans and *Ralliés,* believes that the Republic such as it is will last. Some dream of a socialist Republic, others of a Catholic Republic, and others of a Caesarian Republic. As for the parliamentary Republic, everybody, even those who have exploited it for the last fifteen years, feel that it is doomed. Everything indicates that we are in for a struggle between the advocates of the different types of Republics. In this struggle Monarchists will have a great role to play; they will place themselves on the side of order and principle.[36]

---

[35] *La France Nouvelle,* September 27, 1892.
[36] Quoted in *Le Figaro,* June 19, 1893.

Again, as in the past, the Intransigents were willing to lay aside the constitutional question and defend more realistic principles. D'Haussonville implied in his speech before the Monarchist Press Association that it was possible to cooperate with other conservative elements. Nothing, however, would shake them from their honor-encrusted belief in a restoration—not the Pope nor the threat to Conservative unity which the *Ralliement* represented.

Au milieu des sollicitudes was a complete justification of the position taken by the left wing of the *Droite constitutionnelle*. Paul Descottes, head of the Conservatives in Savoy and a member of this group, made it abundantly clear in *Le Figaro* of May 24, 1892 what acceptance to the Republic would involve. "The country must know that you [the *Droite constitutionnelle*] will no longer combat Republican institutions but that you will consider them as forever established and therefore indisputable." The implications of this statement were enormous. The *Ralliés,* as members of the Piou group were now called, would have to accept the laic laws at least for the moment. Piou and the more conservative members of the group were still reluctant to go this far because they knew that it would end forever any possibility of further cooperation with the Intransigents and because they knew that acceptance to this extent might antagonize many Catholics.

In a speech delivered shortly after the publication of the encyclical, Thellier de Poncheville attempted to interpret the Pope's sentiments in a way which would not exclude association with the extreme Right. He said, "We must unite on the basis of the right to defend religious and social peace." This statement was certainly compatible with the program of the newly formed *Union de la droite libérale.* De Poncheville then proceeded to attack the laic laws violently but ended with the following paradoxical statement: "We want peace and freedom. On these grounds we will fight for God and country." [37] The deputy

---

[37] Charles Thellier de Poncheville, *Les Catholiques en France* (Châlons-sur-Marne, 1892), pp. 1–11.

from the Nord was trying to reconcile the Vatican's desire for appeasement with the French Catholics' desire to fight Republican legislation. Nowhere in the speech was there a clear-cut statement of adherence to the Republic.

Albert de Mun, the great Catholic statesman, rallied in May 1892 in obedience to the Vatican. His speech before the *Ligue de propagande catholique et sociale* at St.-Étienne in December 1892, reflected the dilemma of the Catholic who did not want to oppose the encyclical and at the same time wanted to vindicate the rights of the Church. De Mun said, ". . . we accept the form but we want to change the substance," and he added that in the next elections Catholics should support only those candidates who would help the Church. There was nothing in the speech which ran contrary to the feelings of the clergy as a whole, but at the end his tone changed. "Gentlemen! Catholics must be the first to extend the hand and cooperate with others, no matter who they are, as long as they want unity of conservative forces. If they do this they are not only doing their duty by obeying the Pope, but also acting as Frenchmen in sacrificing to the public good everything in their program which is too absolute and rigid in order to attract other groups of decent men."[38] The hostile note at the beginning of the speech had changed to one of conciliation.

There was continuing pressure on Jacques Piou to define his position with regard to the Republic in the light of the recent encyclical. On June 12, 1892, *Le Figaro* and the *Observateur Français,* both newspapers which supported the *Ralliement,* announced that the deputy from the Haute-Garonne was about to make a statement which would resolve once and for all the position of the *Droite constitutionnelle.* The long-awaited statement was made in the form of an interview in the Paris edition of the *New York Herald* on June 12, 1892. Piou's reluctance to define the position of his group was indicated by his choice of a relatively obscure newspaper in which to present his views. The *Herald* interview added nothing to what Piou had said previously. He

[38] *L'Observateur Français,* December 21, 1892.

repeated his opinion that the Republic was an established fact and that it should belong to all Frenchmen and not merely to a clique. He said nothing about defending Republican institutions in a time of crisis.

Some felt that Piou was too timid. Dugué de la Fauconnerie, an old associate of Raoul-Duval, suggested this in an article in *L'Éclair* (June 26, 1892), and in some notes he made for a speech given in Bordeaux on July 14, 1892. Étienne Lamy wrote, "He has started too timidly. He does not want to separate himself from the Conservatives." [39] Others were more kindly disposed. In an editorial entitled "A Little Patience Please!" *La France Nouvelle* of March 20, 1892 pointed out that Piou was convinced that the Republic must be adhered to without reservations but that he was moving slowly in order to convince the many wavering Conservatives that the Republic could be squared with their consciences. Piou himself implied this in a letter to the Abbé Gayraud (a Christian Democrat), which appeared in *La France Nouvelle* on August 3, 1892. "How is one to overcome so much sincere resistance and respectable sentiment? How can one easily ask men who have made it a point of honor to defend the hereditary principle and who for sixty years have sacrificed so much for it to change their political views?"

There were three decisive events in 1892 which determined the course of the *Droite constitutionnelle* in the following election year. The first was the publication of the encyclical. The second was the adherence to the Republic of the Baron de Mackau and De Mun—outstanding Conservative leaders—and the resignation of De Breteuil, which was a severe blow to the Intransigents. The third was the formation of an organization known as *La Ligue populaire pour la revendication des libertés publiques*. Its leaders were Gaston David, brother-in-law of Sadi-Carnot, President of

---

[39] These notes are among the unpublished papers of Étienne Lamy which are in the possession of M. Dominique Audollent of Clermont-Ferrand. See Bibliography.

the Republic, and Étienne Lamy, a Catholic Republican. The
League was founded in Bordeaux and according to a dispatch in
L'Observateur Français of March 24, 1892, had departmental
committees in Paris, Lyons, Marseilles, Toulouse, and other provincial cities. Its program included the following: loyal adherence
to the Republic; modification of the *loi scolaire* where it was in
conflict with the rights of the family; the right to associate freely;
fiscal responsibility; and greater freedom for the communes and
departments.[40]

The League did not want to be considered a Catholic organization and based its program on a spirit of liberalism which it hoped
would attract Republican Liberals, chiefly the members of the
Left Center such as Léon Say and Jules Simon. It had in mind the
revival of the old Center before it split on the constitutional question in 1875. According to *Le Figaro* of February 12, 1892, Gaston
David said that the League would not insist upon immediate
revision of the laic laws. "The change would come with time."
The League put itself squarely in the tradition of Raoul-Duval.
Once the Conservatives laid down their arms and joined the Republic, the *raison d'être* of the Republican "bloc" would come to
an end. David's organization was well received by the press which
supported the *Ralliement,* and this must have contributed to
Piou's decision to join forces with it. He and Thellier de Poncheville, together with David and Lamy, organized a series of lectures to publicize the League's program during the summer of
1892.[41]

The new year (1893) brought a rash of statements from Piou
and the *Droite constitutionnelle* showing the influence of the
three events of the preceding year. On January 8, Piou published
an article in *Le Figaro* entitled "*Un programme de la droite
républicaine*." The deputy from the Haute-Garonne argued for

[40] *L'Observateur Français,* February 2, 1892.
[41] *Ibid.,* June 3, 1892.

the creation of a two-party system within the existing constitutional framework, which would pit conservatives against "revolutionaries."

It is for us to organize a truly Republican Conservative party.

No excessive demands, no suspicions or rancorous thoughts, no metaphysical theories or aspirations towards an impossible ideal. We must move fast, having as a program the formation of an honest, open and tolerant Republic.

A month later Piou rose in the Chamber to attack the "bloc" mentality of the Republican majority. He said that the *Droite constitutionnelle* would never become a part of the present majority but added,

If the day ever comes when the majority in the Chamber consists of men who, without making any concessions on issues which I will never cease to support, would apply the *loi scolaire* fairly, if that day comes, we would not refuse these men our support.[42]

This was an extraordinary statement if one considers Piou's reluctance in the previous year to separate himself from the *Union des droites*. What he said in effect was that if a Republican government applied the laic laws justly *without revising them,* the *Droite constitutionnelle* would support it, even though it was committed to a textual revision of these laws. In a speech in Toulouse in April Piou attributed the evolution of his group toward sincere adherence to the Republic to the initiative of the Vatican and the ineffectiveness of the Conservative position.

You ask me why we did not take this step in 1889. I would like to ask my interrogators what they would have done then? 1889 was very different from 1893. Since then a movement has been initiated the high purpose and effectiveness of which will soon be readily apparent.[43]

In the speech, however, he made a final appeal for Conservative unity by insisting once again that the Right could be united if

[42] J. O., Chambre, Débats (February 16, 1893), p. 747.
[43] *L'Observateur Français,* April 28, 1893.

only all Conservatives adhered to the Republic. But as in the case of Raoul-Duval, this appeal fell on deaf ears.

On March 28, the members of the *Droite constitutionnelle* met at the home of Hély d'Oissel and voted to change its name officially to the *Droite républicaine*.[44] The group held a banquet at the Hotel Continental in Paris on June 21, and two hundred people heard the Prince d'Arenberg and Jacques Piou urge the formation of a new and homogeneous majority which would provide the country with the stable government it so desperately needed.[45] After the banquet Piou and his followers set out to prepare for the elections which were to take place on August 21 and September 3.

It would be too much to say that on the eve of the elections the *Droite républicaine* was a "government" group. It was prepared to be, however, if the Opportunists could rid themselves of the "bloc" mentality during the electoral campaign and adopt a tolerant attitude toward the *Ralliés*. This position was very different from the one reflected in the tenuous statements of the group as a whole in 1890, 1891, and even as late as 1892. The *Ralliés* knew that it was hopeless to act in concert with the Intransigents despite Piou's final appeal for Conservative unity at Toulouse in April 1893. Like Raoul-Duval, who found himself in much the same situation in 1886, the *Ralliés* were forced to turn to the Left and advocate the formation of a "Tory" party within the Republican framework. Otherwise they would have had no further *raison d'être* as a political force. The sincerity of their adherence to the Republic is attested to by the fact that it occurred during the Panama Canal crisis which broke at the end of 1892. This crisis provided anti-Republican sentiment with an excellent opportunity to repeat their charge that the regime was rotten and corrupt.

The failure of the *Union des droites* to provide an effective program of action, the policy of the Vatican, and the influence of

[44] *Le Figaro*, March 29, 1893.
[45] *Ibid.*, June 22, 1893.

the *Ligue pour la revendication des libertés publiques* were major factors in directing the political course of the *Droite constitution-nelle*. Another factor of considerable importance was the increased division between Opportunists and Radicals. The Panama crisis aggravated this division and convinced many Opportunists that a more homogeneous majority was needed in order to develop more stable governments. This realization (as the fourth chapter will show) coincided with Piou's attacks on "concentration" and his demands for a workable majority.

4

Before entering upon a discussion of the elections of 1893, it is necessary to consider briefly a movement among French Catholics which paralleled that of Piou, Lamy, and David and which was to have a great influence both on the *Ralliement* and on the evolution of French Catholicism in the twentieth century. This was the Christian Democratic movement.

The Christian Democratic ideal, which developed in France in the 1890's, was inspired by three events. The first was the formation in the 1870's of *L'Oeuvre des cercles* under the leadership of Albert de Mun and the Marquis da la Tour du Pin. Although both men were Royalists, they were anxious to put the Church in touch with the problems created by industrialization and to meet the challenge of socialism. *L'Oeuvre des cercles* involved workers' study groups which looked into various problems of immediate interest to the working classes. The movement was popular among the workers in Paris, in the north and in the south-west during the 1880's, but it dwindled in the 1890's when socialism became widespread.[46]

The second event was the publication in 1891 of *Rerum novarum,* in which the Vatican took up the social question for

[46] The definitive work thus far on Social Catholicism in France in this period is Henri Rollet, *L'Action sociale des catholiques en France 1871–1901* (Paris, 1947). See also Parker T. Moon, *The Labor Problem and the Social Catholic Movement in France* (New York, 1921).

the first time. This famous encyclical resulted from the efforts of De Mun and De la Tour du Pin in France, Cardinal Manning in England, Bishop Ketteler in Germany, and the Baron von Vogelsang in Austria, all of whom were interested in this problem. In *Rerum novarum* Leo XIII commiserated with the plight of the working class and pointed out once again that only the Church could provide an effective solution to social questions. The key to such a solution was charity—charity which should pervade the spirit of the entrepreneurial class and the government. In certain instances, it was right for a government to interfere on behalf of the proletariat in order to ensure better living conditions. Comparing this statement with the *Syllabus of Errors,* one can see how anxious Leo XIII was to bring the Church to grips with the modern world.

The third event which influenced the development of Christian Democracy was the encyclical *Au milieu des sollicitudes.* Together with *Rerum novarum* this document seemed proof to many young Catholics, both lay and clerical, that the spirit of democracy had reached the Vatican.

The leaders of the movement were the Abbés Gayraud, Naudet, Garnier, Didon, Lemire, and Dabry, and among the laymen, Georges Goyau, Jean Brunhès, and Léon Harmel. They were, for the most part, bright young priests and laymen who had reached maturity under the Third Republic and were not interested in the chimeric possibility of a restoration.[47] They were profoundly democratic and believed that the principles of the French Revolution could benefit the Church. In this belief they differed sharply from De Mun and De la Tour du Pin.

The Christian Democrats represented a minority within the French Church, but the political events of the 1890's were to give them both impetus and publicity. Christian Democracy was particularly strong in the north, where the *Oeuvres des cercles* had

[47] Lecanuet, *L'Église de France sous la Troisième République,* II, 461–465; Dansette, *Histoire religieuse de la France contemporaine,* II, 199–201.

taken root. In the department of the Nord workers and priests formed the *Union démocratique du Nord* in 1892, and during the same year a review, *La Démocratie Chrétienne,* was established in Lille. The movement expanded throughout France, and in 1893 the Christian Democrats held their first Congress in Rheims.[48]

For Christian Democracy *Au milieu des sollicitudes* and *Rerum novarum* together formed a political program. The *Ralliement* was not "simply a change of label but a renovation of political habits."[49] Catholics were not going to defend conservative principles under the Republic but were going to bring the Church to the people. Catholics were not going to defend vested interests but were going to offer the people an alternative to socialism. In the first edition of the Abbé Naudet's *Justice Sociale,* founded in Bordeaux on July 15, 1893, the following statement appeared:

This newspaper is born of Faith, of the feeling of profound devotion for the people, and of the generous help of friends.

We believe that it responds to a need and we hope it will be well received.

On the one hand, serious and honest workers ask us to help them defend their professional interests. They are sick of Socialist pamphlets which mix a few good grains with a great deal of chaff. They reject those who seek to divide the great French family into two hostile camps. On the other hand, there are a number of people with legitimate grievances and who would like to ease their consciences through the study of economic and social questions.

La Justice Sociale hopes to respond to this double need. This is our editorial position. We are Catholics, devoted children of the Church, who love and respect its authority and who submit to its teachings.

We have read the Gospel and we have heard the great voice of the Father of the Faithful.

The Gospel has shown us the compassion that Jesus showed to all who suffer. It has engraved on our hearts the charitable words fallen from those divine lips.[50]

[48] Lecanuet, *L'Église de France,* II, 455.
[49] Pierre Dabry, *Les Catholiques républicains 1890–1903* (Paris, 1905), p. 121.
[50] Quoted in Robert Cornillau, *L'Abbé Naudet* (Paris, 1935), pp. 47–48.

The differences between the Christian Democrats and the *Droite républicaine* were profound, and they were to affect the course of the *Ralliement* after the elections of 1893, when the Christian Democrats were stronger and better organized. Piou and his followers accepted the Republic in order to defend vested interests; the Abbé Naudet and Goyau accepted the Republic because they were basically democratic. On the other hand, the Christian Democrats were more clerical in their political approach than was the *Droite républicaine*. Christian Democracy was a crusade to bring the popular classes back to the Church, and many priests were associated with the movement. This spirit is reflected in a statement made by the Abbé Naudet after the elections.

The important question today is not whether there are more Opportunists, Radicals, Royalists and *Ralliés* in the Chamber. The question is whether there are still some valiant souls left who are not exhausted, who are not devoid of conviction and who are prepared to fight.

Everything is ready, my friends. Take stock of the situation and then stand up. God does not die.[51]

The tone was militant, and in this it resembled the appeals of other French Catholics who were less enthusiastic about the Republic. But even though the Christian Democrats did cooperate with the other *Rallié* groups in preparing for the coming elections, it was clear that there was no real basis for an understanding.[52]

5

The elections of 1893 provided a critical test for the *Ralliement*. If there were any doubts about the Vatican's conciliatory policy toward the Third Republic after the encyclical of 1892, they were dispelled on August 3, 1893, by a letter from the Pope to Cardinal Lecot. This letter (published in *Le Temps* of August

[51] Quoted in *ibid.*, p. 61.
[52] J.-Ph. Heuzey-Goyau, *Georges Goyau* (Paris, 1947), pp. 134–135. See also Cornillau, *L'Abbé Naudet*, p. 35.

14, 1893) was written in response to a statement of the Cardinal which suggested provisional acceptance of the laic laws. The Pope said:

> We appeal to all French citizens, men of justice and courage, to recognize and guard loyally the constitution of the country as it exists. We ask them to forget old quarrels and to work energetically to instill justice and equity in the laws to the end that respect and true liberty will be given the Church. Thus through a spirit of fraternity these men will provide prosperity to the nation to which they are all devoted.

Thus, on the eve of the elections, Leo XIII reiterated the need for cooperation between Catholics and moderate Republicans. This definitive statement coincided with the conciliatory gestures of the *Droite républicaine*.

The *Droite républicaine* and the *Ligue pour la revendication des libertés publiques* offered approximately ninety-four candidates.[53] Although the *Ralliés* had made it clear that they would not cooperate with the Intransigents, they did not challenge their former colleagues in the areas where royalism and Catholicism were strongest—the five Breton departments and the Vendée. In these departments a Conservative who was not a noble and an outspoken defender of religious interests did not stand a chance of election. Departments such as the Sarthe, Eure, Loire-Inférieure, and Mayenne in which the *Ralliement* did offer candidates also had strong conservative traditions, but these were less intimately associated with past regimes. Although part of the conservative west, they were less cut off from the mainstream of political life than was Brittany.[54] There were also *Rallié* candidates in the north and the southwest and in the departments along the Loire, industrial and agricultural regions where eco-

---

[53] Henri Avenel, *Comment vote la France, 18 ans de suffrage universel* (Paris, 1894), p. 26.

[54] André Siegfried, *Tableau politique de la France de l'ouest* (Paris, 1913), p. 230.

nomic and social realities did much to convert Conservatives to the regime. Here the *Ralliés* were able to appeal to the traditionally conservative vote, and at the same time they could expect the support of the Catholics.[55]

Most of the *Rallié* candidates were either industrialists or large landowners (see appendix B). A typical example of their political viewpoint was the *profession de foi* of Baron des Rotours, an industrialist from the Nord, which appeared in *La Dépêche du Nord* on August 13, 1893. ". . . I have never involved myself in the discussion of irritating problems in the Chamber. Rather I have devoted myself to the study of economic and financial questions the solution of which will produce pacification, concord and peace." Another example was provided by the Prince d'Arenberg, a large landowner from the Cher and one of the directors of the Suez Company, who, in his statement to the voters, urged the new legislature to "undertake with resolution a study of the social question."[56]

Many *Ralliés* never brought up the subject of the laic legislation in their *professions de foi*. Of the thirty-five candidates elected, only twelve had discussed it (see appendix B). Most contented themselves with rather vague statements. That of Le Gavrien, another industrialist from the Nord appeared in *La Dépêche du Nord* on August 12: "I would like to see a liberal and tolerant Republic open to everyone of good faith, economic in its public spending, honest, and merciless with regard to speculators." Achille Fould, member of one of France's leading banking families and deputy from the Hautes-Pyrénées,

[55] Report of the departmental prefects in Brittany to the Ministry of Public Worship on the influence of the clergy and of the Catholic press on the elections of 1893. A. N. F19 5619.

[56] *Rapport fait au nom de la Commission chargée de réunir et de publier les textes authentiques des programmes et engagements électoraux des députés. Sixième législature* (Paris, 1894), p. 184. L. Arthur Minnich emphasizes the influence of economic and social issues as a whole on the elections of 1893 in his essay "The Third Force, 1870–96," in Edward M. Earle, ed., *Modern France* (Princeton, 1951), pp. 109–123.

stated in *La Liberté des Hautes-Pyrénées* on August 18, "We are partisans of a wise and moderate Republic."

A larger number of *Rallié* candidates called for a Republican government supported by a homogeneous majority. This conformed to the desires of the Vatican and the *Droite républicaine* to cooperate with the conservative Republicans. Jacques Piou, in a letter to the voters of the Haute-Garonne, published in *La Dépêche du Nord* of August 29, called once again for a union of *"les hommes de l'ordre"* against the Radicals who sought to destroy France. Where it was possible for a *Rallié* to throw his support to an Opportunist on the second ballot, he did so.[57] Léon Renard, a *Rallié* candidate from the Nord, wholeheartedly endorsed the Opportunist platform in a statement appearing in *La Dépêche du Nord* of August 29. "The Republic of Cavaignac, Constans, Casimir-Perier and Jonnart, as reflected in their recent statements, is the basis for our unity."

But although the *Ralliés* were anxious to cooperate with the Opportunists, the latter were not interested. When Jean Casimir-Perier, future President of the Republic, talked about homogeneous majorities during the campaign, calling them ". . . the only ones capable of serving the country within and without and of realizing those reforms legitimately demanded by the spirit of democracy," [58] this did not include the *Ralliés*. The election returns published in *Le Temps* (August 22 and September 5) for the balloting of August 21 and September 3 show that approximately three quarters of the *Rallié* candidates were opposed by Opportunists. The *Dépêche du Nord* complained on August 7, "The Opportunist press is going out of its way to present a distorted picture of the liberal candidates we support." Piou said that the prefect of the Haute-Garonne supported his Radical opponent.[59] De Vogüé, the *Rallié* candidate in the Ardèche,

[57] *Le Temps*, September 5, 1893.

[58] Quoted in Alphonse Bertrand, *La Chambre de 1893* (Paris, 1894), p. 58.

[59] *L'Univers*, September 10, 1893.

claimed that this was also true for his department;[60] and in the Haute-Savoie, Descottes complained that he got no official support despite his firm adherence to existing institutions.[61] According to *Le Temps* of September 5, there were a few instances where an Opportunist threw his support to a *Rallié* on the second ballot, but in general they were not eager to accept the followers of Piou and Lamy as full-fledged Republicans.

There were not many cases where *Rallié* candidates opposed the extreme Right. Although the *Droite républicaine* and Gaston David's league did not challenge monarchist sentiment in Brittany or in the Vendée, *Rallié* candidates did oppose Monarchists and Bonapartists in two departments bordering on Brittany. In the Maine-et-Loire, Georges de Grandmaison defeated a Bonapartist, and in the Loire-Inférieure, Amaury Simon defeated a Monarchist. A classic example was in the Gers, in the southwest, where a *Rallié* candidate threw his support to a Radical who then went on to defeat Paul de Cassagnac, the outspoken representative of the Intransigent position in the Chamber.

The Christian Democrats presented only one candidate. In the Nord, the Abbé Lemire ran against a field which included a candidate of the *Droite républicaine,* General Frescheville. Lemire was alarmed by the General's conservative views, which he knew would be unpopular with the voters in Hazebrouck, a working-class district.[62] However, although the Abbé's *profession de foi,* which appeared in *La Dépêche du Nord* on August 15, reflected a more enthusiastic acceptance of the Republic, it was far more critical of the laic legislation. "I am against divorce, which is an example of Jewish influence on the legislature. I am against the restrictions placed on religious associations, the school without God, and service in the field required of *curés.*" On the other hand, Frescheville had told the voters that religious

[60] *Ibid.,* September 15, 1893.
[61] *Ibid.,* September 10, 1893.
[62] Henry Carnoy, *Dictionnaire des hommes du Nord* (Paris, 1899), p. 21.

questions were becoming less acute.[63] The conservative *Dépêche du Nord,* which supported *Droite républicaine* candidates, was outraged by what it regarded as Lemire's intrusion in Haze-brouck, and it refused to support him on the second ballot when Frescheville withdrew. But Frescheville's support went to the Abbé anyway, and he defeated the Opportunist candidate. The Hazebrouck election was an indication of the divergent positions taken by the *Droite républicaine* and the Christian Democrats.

Thirty-six *Ralliés* were elected to the Chamber in 1893[64] as opposed to fifty-eight Intransigents. The three leaders of the *Ralliement,* Piou, De Mun, and Lamy, were defeated by Republicans. Twenty-four *Rallié* deputies came from the north and the fringe areas of the west, and the remaining twelve were scattered through the center and the southwest.

The elections of 1893 marked the destruction of the *Union des droites.* Once again the Conservatives failed to act as an effective political force. In the Gers election *Ralliés* would not associate with Intransigents, even if it meant the election of a hated Radical. The possibility of unifying the Right had vanished. Strongly royalist and Catholic Brittany could not be induced to place itself upon constitutional terrain despite pressure from the Vatican and the threat of division. Because the *Ralliés* were the only Conservative candidates in certain departments, the Church supported them (although their stand on religious issues was not all that the Church expected).[65] The *Ralliés* on their own could not be considered a political force. If they had seriously thought that

[63] *La Dépêche du Nord,* August 4, 1893.

[64] It is difficult to arrive at an exact figure. Some *Ralliés* were listed as Conservatives, others as Republicans. Some Intransigents were classified as *Ralliés.* *L'Univers* (September 5) listed 51 elected *Ralliés; Le Figaro* (September 5) listed 45; *Le Matin* (September 5) listed 28. A study of the Barodet Report as well as various lists of deputies who were members of the *Droite constitutionnelle* convinces me that there were 36.

[65] Report of the departmental prefects in Brittany to the Ministry of Public Worship on the influence of the clergy and of the Catholic press on the elections of 1893. A. N. F19 5619.

they would receive the overwhelming support of the fundamentally conservative electorate by accepting the Republic, the election returns shattered this illusion.

The winners of the elections were the Opportunists. They emerged with 311 seats to 122 for the Radicals and 49 for the Socialists.[66] It was they, and not the followers of Piou, who were the beneficiaries of the *Ralliement*. "The Republic has penetrated into the last fortresses of the reactionaries. She has regained the Ille-et-Villaine, part of Finistère, a seat or two in the Loire-Inférieure, in the Vendée and in Gers . . . It is the moderates who have triumphed." *Le Temps* of August 22, 1893 implied that the policy of the Vatican had produced votes for the Opportunists. This is substantiated by André Siegfried, who has pointed out that in times of appeasement Republicans made considerable gains in Conservative areas.[67]

With the Opportunists firmly in control, the success of the *Ralliement* would now depend upon whether the *Droite républicaine* could make the Opportunists realize that it was in their best interests to create a homogeneous majority which would include the *Ralliés*. Its success also depended upon whether the vast majority of Catholics would accept the long-term policy laid down by the Vatican. On November 14, shortly after the elections, Ernest Daudet wrote in *Le Figaro*, "We must show that we are not opposed to the government. We will energetically support ministries which reject Radical support. We will not haggle over this support." This implied that the followers of Jacques Piou were willing to create a climate in the Chamber which would facilitate the formation of a new political alliance between the Opportunists and the *Droite républicaine*.

[66] *Le Temps,* September 8, 1893. See also Goguel, *La Politique des partis,* p. 72.
[67] Siegfried, *Tableau politique,* pp. 466, 470.

CHAPTER III
The Ralliement
1894-1898

During the first phase of the *Ralliement* (1890–1893) the focus of attention was on the Conservatives. The movement was begun not by Cardinal Lavigerie's toast, but by the formation of the *Droite constitutionnelle*. Lavigerie and Leo XIII were taking advantage of the ferment within the Right which had resulted from the Boulanger crisis in order to change the political orientation of the French Catholics. This was quite natural, for the Catholics had traditionally been associated with the Conservatives. Although there were certain indications of independent action between 1890 and 1893, Catholics generally maintained these ties. During the second phase of the *Ralliement* (1894–1898) the focus shifted from the Conservatives to the Catholics. The significant aspect of this phase was the effort made by Catholics both in France and in Rome to coordinate Catholic political activity in view of the elections of 1898. What were the reasons for this shift?

In 1894 the *Rallié* deputies decided to call themselves "Independent Republicans," and they selected as their leader Le Gavrien (Nord) to replace Jacques Piou, who was no longer a deputy. According to their *professions de foi* of the previous year and subsequent statements which appeared in the *Rallié* press, these deputies were willing to support those ministries which reflected religious appeasement and respect for law and order. At the same time they wanted to make it clear that they were not absolutely committed to supporting the government. The *Ralliés* hoped that they could use their 36 votes in the chamber in such a way as to influence both the Intransigents and the Opportunists.

The idea that the former could somehow be enticed into reorganizing the *Union des droites* within the framework of the Republic had not died out despite every indication that the Intransigents would never go so far. At any rate the change in the name of the group from the *Droite républicaine* to the Independent Republicans clearly indicated the intention of the members not to fall completely under the influence of the Opportunists and to maintain some freedom of action. Shortly after the new legislature met, the *Ralliés* issued a statement stressing their continued support for a change in the laic laws in order to give the Church a greater role in primary education.[1]

Despite statements made by the Independent Republicans that they would operate as a cohesive political unit in the Chamber, their actions between December 1893, when the Jean Casimir-Perier ministry was formed, and April 1896, when the Méline ministry came into being, indicated the contrary. The divisions which had hampered the group in determining its precise relationship to the Republic in 1890 and 1892 continued to exist. Yet the parliamentary action of the Independent Republicans revealed that a majority did tend to favor cooperation with Opportunist ministries wherever possible.

On March 3, 1894 Eugène Spuller, Minister of Public Worship in the Casimir-Perier ministry and close friend and associate of Léon Gambetta, rose to his feet to denounce the "sectarian spirit" which had been so harmful to a good working relationship between the government and the Catholic Church until 1893.

> I say that on this point you can count on the vigilance of the Government in its defense of the rights of the State, and, at the same time, you can also count on a new spirit [*esprit nouveau*] which will guide its actions in this defense and which will serve to reconcile all citizens . . .[2]

---

[1] L. Bouvattier, "La Droite républicaine dans la chambre nouvelle," *Le Figaro*, April 24, 1894. See also *L'Univers*, June 9, 1894.

[2] J. O., Chambre, *Débats* (March 3, 1894), p. 483.

This conciliatory statement on the part of a Republican minister provoked a sharp attack from the Radicals, led by Henri Brisson. At the conclusion of the debate the Chamber was asked to support the government in an *ordre du jour* framed by the Opportunist Louis Barthou.

The Chamber, confident of the desire on the part of the Government to maintain the laws of the Republic and to defend the rights of the State, passes to the order of the day.[3]

Albert de Mun, who had recently been re-elected in a by-election in the Morbihan, pointed up a dilemma confronting the Independent Republicans. If Barthou's *ordre du jour* meant that he and his associates would have to vote for the laic laws and the government, then he, as a Catholic, could not do it. If, on the other hand, the *ordre du jour* called for support of a ministry which was prepared to apply a new spirit to religious problems, then he could support it. Because he could not decide what it called for, De Mun abstained.[4] Two hundred and eighty deputies voted for the resolution, and one hundred and twenty voted against it. Among the Independent Republicans, thirteen approved it, and seventeen abstained from voting. Four Independent Republicans were absent.[5] The majority refused to associate themselves with the *ordre du jour* for fear of being misunderstood on the question of the laic laws. Only Lemire, the Christian Democrat, and the *Rallié* deputy from the Nord, Montalembert, opposed the resolution.

The Independent Republicans supported the Casimir-Perier ministry more often than not, despite their reservations on the question of the *"esprit nouveau."* They voted for the government when it was overthrown on May 22,[6] and they supported the

[3] J. O., Chambre, *Débats*, p. 489.
[4] *Ibid.*, p. 489.
[5] *Ibid.*, p. 495.
[6] *Ibid.* (May 22, 1894), p. 319.

succeeding Dupuy ministry (May 1894–January 1895) because it was also composed, for the most part, of Opportunists.[7]

One of the great issues which was to affect church-state relations in the 1890's and, more particularly, the course of the *Ralliement* came to the fore in March 1895. It arose during the prolonged debate on the budget for 1895 when the government, then headed by Alexandre Ribot (an Opportunist) attempted to readjust a tax which had been levied on certain associations, civil and religious, but which affected religious orders more than others. The original tax, known as the *droit d'accroissement,* was the result of two laws passed in 1880 and 1884. It levied a certain sum upon each monastic order every time one of its members died, on the assumption that the order was that much richer because of the reduction in its numbers. This tax had always been unpopular with the Catholics because it supposedly violated the principal of *mainmorte,* and it was also unpopular with the government because it was difficult to figure the rate of assessment on each order each time a member died. Thus when the Ribot ministry, formed in January 1895, came to determine the budget for that year, it decided to change the tax to an annual assessment of each order, authorized and unauthorized, of thirty centimes on 100 francs. This made it much easier to collect. The new tax, known as the *droit d'abonnement,* evoked a violent protest from the Catholics, who felt that the tax was much too high and too great an infringement on Church property. For those Catholics and Intransigents who were always eager to find an excuse to attack the Republic, the *droit d'abonnement* was made to order as an issue. For those who were making every effort to find some grounds for cooperation with the Republic, it was a difficult moment.[8]

[7] *Ibid.* (January 11, 1895), p. 84. See also Goguel, *La Politique des partis,* pp. 72–73.

[8] Dansette, *Histoire religieuse de la France contemporaine,* II, 241–246. See also Ferrata, *Ma Nonciature en France,* pp. 486–492.

The debates on the question took place in the Chamber on March 18, 19, and 20, 1895. On March 18, the Intransigents offered an amendment which would eliminate the tax altogether, and in this they received the support of the *Ralliés* with the exception of the Comte d'Alsace, a recently elected deputy from the Vosges. This amendment was easily defeated by the combined efforts of the Republicans.[9]

On the same day another amendment to the proposed law was presented to the Chamber by Clausel de Coussergues, a Left-Centrist deputy from the Aveyron. This amendment was conceived with the help of the Independent Republicans.[10] It called for application of the tax to all associations, civil and religious, and for a reduction from thirty centimes per hundred francs to twenty centimes for authorized orders. It also called for exemptions from the tax for all orders engaged in charitable work.[11] Ribot agreed to the application of the tax to all associations, and he agreed to exemptions for only those orders which were authorized. He refused however to allow precise exemptions to be written into the law, preferring to have a given ministry use its own discretion in the matter. He would not hear of a reduction in the assessment, and when the debate came to a close on March 19, the tax was increased to fifty centimes per hundred francs for unauthorized orders, and thirty centimes per hundred francs for those that were authorized.[12]

These debates gave vent to furious attacks on Republican policy by the Intransigents. It was they, and not the Independent Republicans, who appeared to be upholding the rights of the Church. Although the *Ralliés* voted with the Monarchists on the first amendment and helped Clausel de Coussergues in the framing of his, they did not participate actively in the debates. They

[9] J. O., Chambre, *Débats* (March 18, 1895), p. 1260.
[10] *L'Union Nationale de Bordeaux,* March 20, 1895. This newspaper was founded in 1894 to support the *Ralliement.*
[11] J. O., Chambre, *Débats* (March 18, 1895), p. 1252.
[12] *Ibid.* (March 19, 1895), pp. 1264–1265.

entered in only at the conclusion of the discussion of the budget
as a whole. Then Le Gavrien announced, as president of the
group, that he and his associates would oppose the budget as
a whole on the grounds of increased government spending.[13]
Here was further evidence of the fact that the Independent
Republicans were more concerned with economic problems and
policy than they were with religious matters. Yet their association
with the moderate amendment of De Coussergues suggested that
they were trying to avoid a situation which could prove extremely harmful to the *Ralliement*.

The *droit d'abonnement* crisis provoked considerable protest
from French Catholics both lay and clerical. Many bishops refused to recognize the tax and advocated a policy of passive
resistance on the part of the orders.[14] This kind of agitation led
to a Radical interpellation in the Chamber on July 12, 1895. Once
again the various parliamentary groups were presented with the
opportunity to air their views on the religious situation. An *ordre
du jour* adopted by the Ribot ministry called for defense of the
rights of the State and civil authority in general. In the division
that followed, five *Ralliés* voted with the government, thirteen
against, eight abstained, and ten were fortunate enough to be
on vacation, thereby avoiding a difficult situation.[15] Only half
the Independent Republican deputies present were willing to
oppose the ministry although it reflected "concentration" far
more than its predecessors[16] and was relatively unfriendly toward
the French Church.

In November 1895 Léon Bourgeois replaced Ribot as prime
minister. For the first time in the history of the Third Republic
a Radical ministry came into being. The chief concern of the
cabinet was to reform the antiquated tax structure by introducing
the progressive income tax. Bourgeois could hardly be considered

[13] *Ibid.*, pp. 1340–1341.
[14] Dansette, *Histoire religieuse de la France contemporaine*, II, 243.
[15] J. O., Chambre, *Débats* (July 12, 1895), p. 947.
[16] Goguel, *La Politique des partis*, p. 74.

a socialist, but his ministry did have the support of the Socialist group in the Chamber. This appalled French conservative opinion, Republican and Intransigent alike. "We do not live in peaceful or normal times," announced *Le Figaro* on April 9, 1896.

On the one hand one finds the *enragés,* the monomaniacs who breathe destruction, whose lives are devoted to pitting one class of society against another. This faction is best represented by Jean Jaurès whose entire cause is based on hatred.

On the other hand there are the true liberals whose hearts go out to the oppressed. These people are not reactionaries. They love mankind more than the Socialist demagogues do. They desire only peace and freedom.

When the Bourgeois ministry fell in April 1896, it was replaced by one that was solidly Opportunist in character and led by the agricultural expert, Jules Méline. Conservative deputies on both sides of the constitutional question were convinced that the survival of this ministry was essential in order to save France from anarchy. *L'Univers* of November 24, 1896 commented, ". . . the Independent Republicans, supported by their newspapers, and the Monarchists, despite theirs, are giving the same support to M. Méline that the Socialists gave to Bourgeois."

The Méline ministry lasted from April 1896 until June 1898— longer, at that point, than any other ministry in the history of the Third Republic. It was invariably supported by conservatives of all shades. If there had been any hesitancy on the part of some Independent Republicans to support Opportunist ministries unconditionally, it had disappeared. Their attitude was best expressed by the Prince d'Arenberg in reply to Radical attacks on the ministry for receiving right-wing support. "I will tell you what we *Ralliés* want. It is not high places in the government or public honors of any kind. It is rather to help unify a divided nation and protect her from sterile agitations. What we wish to do is to fortify the ranks of those who fight on the side of order and liberty against the increasing strength of Socialism, which threatens the country with eternal disorder." [17]

On the eve of the elections of 1898 the Independent Republicans were virtually absorbed into the Opportunist majority. [18] The agreement reached by the Opportunists and Independent Republicans in Lille and published in the *Dépêche du Nord* on March 3, 1898 was an example of the new relationship between the two groups. "The committee of Republicans of Government [Opportunists] and the committee of Liberal Republicans consider that it is essential to unite in order to combat the revolutionary Socialist and Radical parties. They desire to contribute to the formation of a great Government party which will assure political and social order, tolerance and religious appeasement to the country." The pact concluded with a promise to support a single list of candidates. The *Dépêche du Nord,* which had complained bitterly of the lack of Opportunist cooperation in 1893, admitted on March 21, 1898 that some concessions had to be made, by which it meant that the agreement with the Opportunists did not include a reform of the laic laws. "Yes, we were forced to make concessions, but the results obtained were much greater and represent a real step forward. The agreement guarantees us peace."

On January 23, 1894, there appeared in the Catholic newspaper *L'Univers* an article entitled, *"Les Ralliés"* which began, "What are the *Ralliés* doing in the Chamber? Does the group have a leader? Does it have a plan of action? Are they prepared to be Catholics above all? Is their battle cry *'Vive l'Église! Vive la France!'?"* The article gave the distinct impression that the *Ralliés* were not sufficiently committed to the interests of the Church. They were not, it claimed, using their votes in the

---

[17] Quoted in Jacques Piou, *Le Ralliement, son histoire* (Paris, 1928), pp. 63–64.

[18] *Ibid.*, pp. 66–67. See also André Reille, *Avant la bataille* (Notre-Dame de Montligeon, 1897), p. 10. Reille was an Independent Republican deputy. See also Shapiro, "The Ralliement in the Politics of the 1890's," p. 42.

Chamber to further religious interests. This was written only four months after the elections of 1893, when the sixth legislature had scarcely had time to reveal its characteristics. The doubts expressed by the editorialist in *L'Univers* about the capacity and ability of the Independent Republicans pervaded Catholic opinion throughout the period between 1894 and 1898.

A number of reasons were offered for the *Ralliés'* disappointing performance. One was that they were suspect to both Republican and Intransigent, which made it difficult to contract effective alliances. The *Rallié* deputies were not attractive enough politically to overcome this suspicion, nor were they able to offer a program that had any extraordinary appeal for other conservative groups. They were accused of trying to develop Royalist ideas under the cover of the *Ralliement* by those who felt that Piou, De Mackau, and De Mun, despite recent utterances, were still compromised by the Boulanger affair.[19] Another criticism leveled against them was that they seemed to be unable to take advantage of the *"esprit nouveau."* *L'Union nationale de Bordeaux* of January 12, 1895, commenting on the political developments of 1894, had this to say:

Despite the excessive optimism of some observers, the past year has brought little improvement in the religious situation. There was, of course, the *"esprit nouveau"* speech of M. Spuller, and several generous statements of M. Viger [Minister of Public Worship in the second Dupuy ministry] but that doesn't amount to much . . .

There is the insolent statement of M. Casimir-Perier on March 3, 1894, which described the laic laws as intangible and part of the patrimony of the Republic and which reaffirmed the "definitive victory of temporal over spiritual authority."

Another editorial written on June 2, 1896, a year after the *droit d'abonnement* crisis, voiced this criticism:

[19] A.-J. Bessières, "Les Ralliés," *L'Univers,* December 4, 1896. See also Boniface de Castellane, "Une equivoque politique; les ralliés," *Nouvelle Revue,* 105:489–498 (April 1897).

Among the causes which have been aggravating the political situation for the past four or five years is the singularly timid and self-effacing attitude of those Catholic deputies who, out of common sense, for practical reasons, or because of the attitude of the Vatican, have placed themselves on Republican terrain. The epithet *"Rallié"* seems to have petrified them, so great is the power of words among us. There seems to be no energy, activity or life of any kind left in them. Instead of seizing upon every opportunity to explain before the Chamber of Deputies the noble reasons which brought them to the Republic, instead of appealing to patriotism and the future of Christian civilization, they give the impression of being ashamed. They leave it to the Catholic newspapers to carry on the struggle. They seem to concern themselves with the personal or electoral ramifications of their position rather than with their obligation to bring about a change in the policy of the government.

A final reason why the *Ralliés* in the Chamber became an increasingly insignificant element in the *Ralliement* after 1894 was the fact that Leo XIII no longer counted on them to bring the movement to fruition. The Pope had insisted that the benefits that Catholics would derive from the *Ralliement* would come when passions on both sides had simmered down. The key to the movement, from his point of view, was a spirit imbued with patience and moderation—an approach which the *Ralliés* in the Chamber accepted. Had the results of the elections of 1893 done anything to alter the opinion of the Pope?

On January 30, 1895, a month before the debates on the *droit d'abonnement,* Cardinal Rampolla, papal Secretary of State, wrote to Auguste Roussel, editor of the intransigent Catholic newspaper *La Verité,*

The Holy Father in innumerable statements has made it clear that French Catholics should place themselves upon constitutional ground and loyally accept the existing form of government. As their influence in politics increases, they will be able to prevent new attacks on the Church, and as a result there will be a gradual amelioration of those laws which are hostile to the Church.

This program, given the difficulty of the situation, calls for assiduous, slow and confident action analogous to a good doctor's treatment of a patient.[20]

Unlike many French Catholics who looked for immediate re-sults from the Spuller announcement of a "new spirit," the Holy See recognized the difficulties facing any Republican government attempting to make textual changes in existing anticlerical legis-lation. "The Vatican understands how difficult is is for the pres-ent Chamber to realize the *'esprit nouveau,'*" wrote Monsignor Mourey, Auditor of the Rota, to his intimate friend Étienne Lamy on April 1, 1894. "It understands the need for a large amount of good will on the part of French Catholics toward the government, and it wishes that all Catholics make every effort not to compromise the ministry either by compliments or by excessive demands."[21]

Leo XIII refused to become involved in the controversy of 1895 over the tax on the monastic orders. According to a letter written by Mgr. Mourey to Étienne Lamy on November 26, 1896, he was embarrassed by the attitude of those French bishops who advocated resistance to the tax.[22] Specifically, he took the position that it was up to the individual bishop to determine his own position on the question because it was a diocesan matter and because it involved direct negotiations between each bishop and the government in determining the assessment. The bishops were advised in a letter (written on May 5 and published in *L'Univers* on May 10, 1895) from Cardinal Rampolla to Cardinal Meignan, Archbishop of Tours, to act with moderation and to attempt to reach a uniform approach to the problem. The above examples indicate that there was no basic change in the Vatican's policy of patience and moderation. The Pope was as eager as the most enthusiastic *Rallié* deputies to maintain good relations with the various Opportunist ministries. There were other reasons why the Holy See decided to veer away from the Independent Republicans after 1894.

[20] Quoted in *L'Univers*, February 4, 1895.
[21] Lamy papers (see Bibliography).   [22] *Ibid.*

Leo XIII was well aware of the rather tarnished political reputations of the *Ralliés* and knew that the elections of 1893 had produced no leader capable of giving the movement greater impetus.[23] But a more compelling reason for the Vatican's decision to look beyond the Chamber for leadership of the *Ralliement* was the proliferation of Catholic organizations throughout France as a result of *Au milieu des sollicitudes*. As these groups multiplied it became essential for them to achieve some kind of political unity. One of the reasons why Leo XIII had advocated the movement was in order to unify Catholic forces. His concern for this problem was reiterated in instructions to French Catholics in 1897 published in *L'Univers* on June 13, 1897. "Catholics must work together closely, putting aside political differences. They must employ all honest and legal means gradually to improve the hostile legislation."

The Christian Democrats, whose primary concern was to bring the Church to the working classes, were particularly active after 1893. The *Abbés démocrates* were convinced that if social reform was necessary it must come from a rejuvenated Church. Between 1894 and 1898 the Christian Democrats held a number of regional and national congresses. They also started several reviews including the *La Démocratie Chrétienne* and *Justice Sociale*.[24]

The group was represented in the Chamber by the Abbé Lemire (deputy from the Nord), who took advantage of every opportunity to defend religious interests. Unlike many of his *Rallié* associates, he refused to support the Casimir-Perier ministry during the debate on the "esprit nouveau" because such support might mean tacit acceptance of the laic laws. Yet on questions of social reform he usually voted with the left.

In January 1897 the Abbé Gayraud, a Christian Democrat, decided to run in the third district of Brest for the seat vacated

[23] Piou, *Le Ralliement*, p. 73.

[24] Maurice Montuclard, "Aux Origines de la démocratie chrétienne," Archives de Sociologie des Religions, 6:47–89 (July–December 1958). See also Henri Rollet, *L'Action sociale des catholiques en France 1871–1901* (Paris, 1947), p. 386.

by the death of Monsignor D'Hulst, rector of the Catholic Institute in Paris. This particular constituency had always been subject to clerical influence and had returned members of the clergy to the Chamber since 1870. D'Hulst's predecessor had been Bishop Freppel of Angers, a leading spokesman for the intransigent Right until his death in 1891. D'Hulst, a childhood friend of the Pretender, the Comte de Paris, had never been able to overcome his monarchist sentiments. The other candidate for the seat in 1897 was a Monarchist, the Comte de Blois. The campaign attracted attention because it pitted a *Rallié* against an Intransigent for the traditionally clerical seat in the Chamber. This bitterly contested election, which the Abbé Gayraud won by twelve hundred votes,[25] was invalidated by a Republican majority in the Chamber because of alleged clerical interference in the campaign;[26] but the Abbé was again elected over Blois in August 1897.

At first glance the significant aspect of the Brest election would seem to be that it represented a *Ralliement* victory. Gayraud enthusiastically accepted the Republic, but like Lemire he insisted upon the abrogation of the laic legislation.[27] His election could, therefore, be viewed as a victory for the aggressive clerical position. It was further indication that if there was a split between priests and aristocrats in the strongly clerical west, the priests were still not about to embrace the Republicans in power. It is not difficult to see why the Republican majority refused to look upon the Abbé as sympathetic to the papal policy of appeasement and conciliation. The Christian Democrats could never accept the conciliatory position of the Independent Republicans toward the anticlerical laws.

Another Catholic organization, formed in response to the *Ralliement,* was the *Union nationale* founded and headed by

[25] Dansette, *Histoire religieuse de la France contemporaine,* II, 251–253.
[26] J. O., Chambre, *Débats* (July 6, 1897), pp. 844–845.
[27] Gayraud's *profession de foi* was quoted in *L'Univers,* January 16, 1897.

the Abbé Garnier. This group was somewhat similar to the
Christian Democrats in that it recognized the need for social
reform and the strengthening of the ties between the clergy and
the popular classes. "We believe," wrote Garnier in *Le Peuple
Français* (organ of the *Union nationale*) on January 6, 1894,
"that the key to the future lies in the solution of the religious,
social and economic problems which confront us. Politics as such
is secondary to this." The *Union nationale* was at the same time
highly nationalist and anti-Semitic. It believed that the decadence
of the nation was due to the Jews, who were sapping her life's
blood.

The Abbé Garnier's organization was not particularly sympathetic with the *Ralliés* in the Chamber because they were not
sufficiently interested in *"la question sociale."* Wrote Garnier in
Le Peuple Français of January 28, 1894, "I respect those Conservatives who are full of good intentions. While admiring these
intentions we must recognize that they have failed." He concluded that there was no reason why the *Union nationale* should
associate itself with the liberal approach of the Independent
Republicans. The followers of the Abbé Garnier, like the Christian Democrats, demanded that the rights of the church be respected, and refused to tolerate anything less than a change in
the laic laws. For this group the *Ralliement* was not a laying
down of arms but a call to battle. Such an attitude hardly coincided with the Vatican policy or that of the Independent
Republicans.

The most powerful single Catholic organization in France at
the end of the nineteenth century was the Assumptionists. At
the heart of this organization was the newspaper *La Croix,*
which was published in Paris but which supported semiautono-
mous editions in the provinces. The paper's great influence was
largely due to the fact that it was prepared to discuss problems
on both the national and local level. In addition to *La Croix,*
the Assumptionists organized a group of political committees

in 1896 throughout the country which were known as *Justice-Égalité*. The political program of these committees included: intransigent opposition to revolutionaries (socialists) and sectarians (Freemasons and Jews); the right to associate freely (a favorite demand of Catholics who wanted unrestricted rights to organize religious groups, which were severely limited by the Concordat and by the Association laws of 1881); administrative decentralization and the right of communities to choose their own primary school teachers.[28]

The Assumptionists refused to recognize the position in which the Catholic Church found itself at the end of the century and were not prepared to meet the challenge of new ideas in the same way as was the Vatican. Leo XIII and the more intellectually sophisticated French Catholics understood that the decreasing influence of the Church posed a serious threat. Hence, *Rerum Novarum*. The Assumptionists, on the other hand, continued in the footsteps of Pius IX. They desired a return to the world of the middle ages where the Catholic Church enjoyed a privileged position.[29] The Assumptionists would accept a Republic if it would put the Church back on its pedestal. They would not, however, accept the Third Republic or the Republicans that governed it. For that reason they found it particularly difficult to follow the advice of the Pope and cooperate with the Opportunists. Father Picard, the head of the order, revealed this in a letter to Leo XIII written in 1893. "Holy Father, they [the Opportunists] are Freemasons. They will betray us. . . . If we do not fight them we will surrender everything to them, and then we will be able to do nothing." [30]

Between 1893 and 1898 the Christian Democrats, the *Union nationale,* and *Justice-Égalité* backed by *La Croix* were the best known Catholic organizations. This was a period, as has been

---

[28] Eugène Jarry, "L'Orientation politique de *La Croix* entre les années 1895–1900," *La Documentation Catholique,* 1154–1049 (August 23, 1954).

[29] *Ibid.,* pp. 1031–1059.

[30] Quoted in *Ibid.,* p. 1042.

said, when Catholics were particularly active in behalf of their own interests. French Catholics had identified their cause with that of the Right until 1892 when it became clear that the *Ralliement* had destroyed the *Union des droites*. Although the Independent Republicans ostensibly represented religious interests in the Chamber, most Catholics realized after the crisis over the tax on the monastic orders, that this parliamentary group was not whole-heartedly committed to the defense of the Church. The Monarchists and the Bonapartists were moribund after 1893, and the Catholics, finding themselves alone, were forced to act on their own initiative. Thus the second phase of the *Ralliement* focused on Catholic rather than Conservative activity.

It was with this situation that the Vatican had to cope. It had to find a means of unifying the various Catholic organizations, most of which were militant in their defense of Church rights, without jeopardizing its policy of appeasement and cooperation with the Opportunists. Although the *Ralliés* in the Chamber were in accord with the policy of the Holy See, they obviously had no influence among the French Catholics as a whole. A new leader had to be found—one who would be respected by Catholics and Republicans alike.

2

In January 1896 Leo XIII summoned Étienne Lamy to Rome. Lamy, it will be remembered, was one of the leaders of the *Ligue pour la revendication des libertés publiques* founded in 1892. He was a Catholic but at the same time an ardent Republican. Born in 1846, he was elected at an early age to the National Assembly in 1871 as a Republican, and he solidified his reputation as such in 1877 by voting with the three hundred and sixty-three deputies against MacMahon's dissolution of the Chamber. Because he was a Catholic, he fell out with the Republican majority during the 1880's when the anticlerical legislation was being enacted. The Pope felt that Lamy's credentials made him the natural leader of the Catholic forces. Nothing is known of Leo XIII's instructions to Lamy during the latter's sojourn in Rome, but a letter from Cardinal Rampolla to Lamy on March 10, 1896, clearly reveals the Vatican's intentions.

Obstacles have made it difficult to realize the benevolent designs of the Sovereign Pontiff with regard to France, chief among which is the lack of organization and unity among well-intentioned citizens which renders them incapable of exercising a salutary influence upon the government and upon the Chambers. Such lack of coordination does nothing but help the enemies of the Church . . . You, sir, will do all in your power to promote unity and organization in Catholic ranks in order to give them a sense of direction, in conformity with the principles laid down by the Holy See. Wherever possible, you will allow each group to maintain its own character and autonomy.[31]

Unlike the Assumptionists, Lamy was well aware that the Catholics in France were in a minority and that Catholic action would have to take this fact into account in order to be successful. His views on the subject appear in a letter which he wrote to Cardinal Langénieux, Archbishop of Rheims, on November 26, 1896:

The pontifical instructions and their slow but continuous influence have rid us of one of the pretexts for anticlericalism. The end of a sterile struggle against the form of government makes it easier for Catholics during future elections to combat more effectively the men and the laws which are hostile to the Church.

But if adherence to the established regime puts Catholics in a better position to continue the struggle against the old Republican party, it does not necessarily assure them of victory. Moreover, the voters, sure of the permanent existence of the Republic, will have to choose between different types of Republics, that is to say between different programs. The success of the Catholic program, therefore, will depend upon the degree to which this program corresponds to the general will.

Catholics must choose between two policies: either to present to the public a picture of the ideal Christian State and demand for the

[31] Lamy papers.

Church all the privileges necessary to fulfill its divine mission, setting the principles of the Church against the ideals of civil society; or to attack this society on its own grounds and demand . . . the cessation of religious persecution in the name of its most cherished principles—liberty, equality, and fraternity.

There would be no reason to contest the validity of the first policy if the majority in a given democracy were Catholic not only by birth but by conviction. But in France at the present time the majority of Citizens are not true Catholics. Thus Catholics can not be expected to help themselves unless they are allied with those elements in the ranks of unbelievers which are honest. These elements have good reason not to associate themselves with Catholics in an effort to restore the Church to its privileged position because by doing this they would be acting contrary to the egalitarian and liberal principles of the Republic. Catholics must appeal to the ideals on which modern society is based in order to vindicate their belief.[32]

This was a classic restatement of the Liberal Catholic position as it had developed in France during the nineteenth century. Montalembert and Lacordaire in their day had based their appeals for a free Church in a free state on the Revolutionary principles of liberty and equality. Lamy's letter to Cardinal Langénieux was a clear indication that the issues which had divided Liberal and Conservative Catholics in the past but which had subsided with the deaths of Bishop Dupanloup and Louis Veuillot in the 1880's were particularly relevant to the second phase of the *Ralliement* when French Catholics were trying to determine a course of action.

Étienne Lamy's problem was to translate Liberal Catholic theory into political practice. The over-all success of the *Ralliement* in the elections of 1898 would depend on the ability of Catholics both to act in unison and to adapt themselves to local situations. Lamy believed that political conditions in a given *arrondissement* should determine whether or not there should

---

[32] A copy of this letter appears in a notebook kept by Lamy entitled "Lettres dont il est utile de prendre copie" in his hand. This notebook will be referred to as the *Cahier*.

be a *Rallié* candidate. If, for example, the *Rallié* had a fair chance of success at the polls, he should present himself as a candidate. If the *Rallié* stood and did poorly on the first ballot, he should then withdraw in favor of an Opportunist candidate on the condition that the Opportunist make some kind of promise reflecting the principle of equal rights for the Church. If the Opportunist refused to make any concessions, then Catholics would feel free to vote, if necessary, for a Royalist.

The precise demands that Catholics would make of Republican candidates also depended upon political conditions on the local level. The strength of the Catholic vote in a given department was the determining factor. Maximum demands, couched, of course, in terms of Republican principles were to include the right for Catholic children to receive religious instruction in primary schools. It was felt that the Catholic child who did not receive this religious instruction was being discriminated against by the laws. The demands also included equal rights for religious associations and equal assessments of both Catholic and lay organizations. Catholics were not to demand a change in the *loi militaire* because it might appear as if they were asking for a privilege.[33]

Lamy assumed, as did many other Catholics after the election of 1893, that Catholic votes had contributed to the success of many Opportunist deputies.[34] This automatically created an obligation on the part of many Republicans toward Catholics who had interpreted the papal instructions in this particular way. Under the influence of this rather tenuous assumption, Lamy began to create a Catholic political organization early in 1896.

In February 1896 the new leader of the *Ralliement* decided to investigate political conditions in various departments. He sent a friend, Charles Denoyel, to sound out Catholic opinion in Lyons, Grenoble, Annecy, Valence, Marseilles, Aix-en-Provence,

---

[33] Lamy's views appear in a copy of a letter which he wrote to the Abbé Pons in Pau in 1896 (no date given), *Cahier,* Lamy papers.

[34] Jarry, "L'Orientation politique," p. 1034.

Millau, the Aveyron, Limoges, and Bourges.[35] Denoyel's mission included seeking out Catholic Republicans, former members of the *Ligue pour la revendication des libertés publiques,* who could head the movement on the local level. Denoyel reported that it was extremely difficult to find potential leaders who were both Catholic and Republican.[36] Catholic *notables* were either tainted by previous political associations or were too clerical in their politics. Denoyel was particularly concerned about the divisions among Catholics. In Grenoble, for example, he found no less than three groups: those who looked to the local *Justice-Égalité* committee for guidance, those who still refused to give up their Royalist convictions, and finally those who were anxious to follow the Vatican's instructions but who were unable to understand the reasons for pursuing a course of action that was not exclusively Catholic.[37] He was impressed by the considerable activity on the part of both the Assumptionists and the *Union nationale* in a number of departments and concluded that it was imperative for Lamy to cooperate with these groups if any sort of Catholic unity was to be achieved.[38]

The most persistent problem that Denoyel encountered during his tour was the strong opposition on the part of many with whom he talked to any real centralization of political activity. Local organizations were particularly jealous of their prerogatives and tended to resent the kind of interference which would become inevitable if a central committee with any kind of authority came into being. According to this point of view, a central Catholic committee would simply serve as a means by which the various local groups could exchange views. It would have no control over their activity.[39]

[35] Denoyel's impressions are recorded in a series of letters which he wrote to Lamy in February and March, 1896 while he was on tour. Lamy papers.

[36] Denoyel to Lamy, Marseilles, February 21, 1896, Lamy papers.

[37] Denoyel to Lamy, Valence, February 27, 1896, Lamy papers.

[38] Denoyel to Lamy, Millau (Aveyron), March 8, 1896, Lamy papers.

[39] Denoyel to Lamy, Lyons, February 22, 1896. See also Denoyel to Lamy, Grenoble, February 24, 1896, and Denoyel to Lamy, Annecy, February 25, 1896, Lamy papers.

With these facts in mind, Étienne Lamy held a meeting at his house in the Place de Jena in Paris on March 26, 1896.[40] It was attended by twenty-seven people, mostly local counsellors and mayors who agreed with their host's ideas. Lamy said that he would respect the autonomy of the various Catholic groups but insisted that a certain amount of central control was necessary if Catholic unity was to be achieved by the elections of 1898. It was decided at the meeting to coordinate the groups at the departmental level and at the same time to sound out non-Catholic sentiment. It was agreed that wherever possible local leaders were to be impeccable Republicans. It was also agreed that the support of the clergy was vital to the success of the movement but that this support would have to be discreet.

Lamy stressed the importance of discretion not only for the priests but for laymen as well. He felt that any kind of purely Catholic political activity would arouse Republican suspicion. For this reason he himself refrained from attending any Catholic meetings or congresses between 1896 and 1898, fearing that it might jeopardize his bargaining position as leader of the *Ralliement* with the Opportunists, who were now solidly in power. It was only at the end of 1897 that his role as leader became known to the public at large.

Throughout 1896 Lamy worked to extend his influence in the various Catholic organizations. He had no difficulty convincing Catholics such as Gaston David and Jules Bonjean who, like himself, were already Republicans. His efforts were endorsed by many Christian Democrats, and Léon Harmel, the titular head of the group, wrote on the eve of the meeting of March 26 that it was imperative for Catholics and other decent men to unite to prepare a better future for the country.[41] The Abbé Naudet, editor of *Justice Sociale*, indicated that he too agreed in general

[40] An account of the meeting of March 26, 1896 appears in a draft of a letter from Lamy to Cardinal Rampolla, March 26, 1896, *Cahier*, Lamy papers.

[41] Léon Harmel to Lamy, March 25, 1896, Lamy papers.

with Lamy's approach.[42] However, the activity of Christian Democrats in that year revealed that there was a considerable difference between themselves and Lamy.

The Christian Democrats organized a congress in Lyons which was held between November 25 and November 30, 1896. It was designed to associate as many Catholics as possible with the idea of social reform and national unity. It attracted many Catholic elements including *La Croix, Justice-Égalité,* and the *Union nationale.* It also attracted Edmond Drumont, editor of the anti-Semitic *Libre Parole.* The central committee of the congress, headed by Mouthon, editor of the Christian Democratic newspaper *La France Libre,* was anxious to have Lamy, as the Vatican-designated head of the *Ralliement,* come to Lyons. Lamy declined the invitation, but he did succeed in obtaining a benediction for the congress from Leo XIII.[43]

The Congress of Lyons was one of two efforts in 1896 to bring Catholics together for a political purpose. All present spoke of the need for unity, but there was not much opportunity for this to be achieved because of the diverse attitudes of the different elements. There was almost no agreement upon how to bring about social reform. Only when the congress attacked the Jews and Freemasons did it show any sign of unity. These attacks merely reflected a continuing hostility toward the Third Republic. No one who desired cooperation with the Opportunists was present at Lyons, neither the Catholic Republicans nor the followers of Jacques Piou, although Piou did send a message to the congress endorsing its general aims. The meeting at Lyons therefore emphasized the herculean task which confronted Lamy in trying to bring a large segment of French Catholic opinion around to his point of view.[44]

[42] Abbé St.-Jean Sentibau to Lamy, March 26, 1896, Lamy papers.

[43] Mouthon to Lamy, October 20, 1896; also Mgr. Mourey to Lamy, October 20, 1896, Lamy papers.

[44] For an account of the Congress of Lyons see *Congrès national de la démocratie chrétienne tenu à Lyon du 25 au 30 novembre 1896, Compte Rendu* (Lyons,

Throughout 1896 the Assumptionists reiterated their eagerness to cooperate with Lamy. "You should know what great pleasure it gave to Father Bailly [editor-in-chief of *La Croix*] and myself to discuss with you the project which you have drawn up with the help of the Vatican," wrote Father Picard, head of the order, to Lamy on August 31, 1896. "We must all work together under the leadership of His Holiness. If we all cooperate, we will have brought into existence a force with which the enemies of the Church will have to reckon.[45] Lamy sought to obtain from Picard the assurance that the order would not draw up an electoral program or make any commitments to candidates without consulting him. Picard assured him that there would be no difficulty in reaching agreement on programs, but he thought that there might be some departments where the local *Justice-Égalité* committees had already pledged their support to candidates.[46] The head of the order was obviously unwilling to place limitations on Assumptionist activities at the local level. The flexibility of departmental committees and editions of *La Croix* were considered the order's greatest assets.

One of the more difficult problems confronting Lamy in 1896 was that of securing the active cooperation of those Catholics who, though they no longer publicly professed allegiance to monarchy or empire, refused explicitly to adhere to the Republic. This had been the attitude of the *Union de la France chrétienne* founded in 1891 in response to Cardinal Lavigerie's toast. The *Union* had considered itself above politics and had relied upon a purely religious program to appeal to all French Catholics. It had been dissolved in 1892 because it was not considered to be thoroughly in line with the Vatican on the question of accepting

---

1896). See also Robert F. Byrnes, "The French Christian Democrats in the 1890's; Their Appearance and their Failure," *Catholic Historical Review*, 36:286–306 (October 1950).

[45] Lamy papers.

[46] Lamy to Mourey, May 17, 1896, *Cahier*, Lamy papers.

the Republic. There were, however, a number of Catholics who continued to maintain an attitude of reserve on this matter.

These hesitant Catholics formed the nucleus of another Catholic congress held in Rheims a month earlier than the one in Lyons to celebrate the fourteen hundredth anniversary of the baptism of Clovis. It offered many conservative Catholics, including the ubiquitous Assumptionists, a chance to air their true feelings about the relationship between Church and State. One particularly popular speech by the Assumptionist Abbé Bouvy contained these words:

> Our beloved France must always be Catholic. She should never forget that she is the eldest daughter of the Church, baptised at Rheims and for centuries the right arm of God. France can be herself only when she adheres to this tradition . . .
>
> We must raise France up again and return her to her faith. We must suck from her breast the poison which is destroying her. We must awaken in her the love of courage and heroism. We must lead her back to her mother, the Church, where once again she will appear joyous and radiant in the light of God.[47]

Another speech delivered by the Abbé Bernard Goudeau of the Catholic Institute in Paris reflected the conservative Catholic attitude even more clearly.

> We must have the courage to admit that intolerance is necessary and legitimate. In the social as well as in the philosophical order of things any organism which has the right to live has the right to be intolerant. The Church want to live. The Church is a mother and there is nothing in the world more legitimately intolerant than a mother. The right to think and to publish one's thoughts without being subject to any rule whatsoever is not in itself a right which the state should support. Free thought is more often than not the cause of much evil . . .[48]

Lamy had been invited to attend the Congress by its president, Thellier de Poncheville, who, it will be remembered, was a

---

[47] Quoted in *Compte rendu général du congrès national de Rheims du 21 au 25 octobre 1896* (Lille, 1897), p. 512.

[48] Quoted in *ibid.*, pp. 186–187.

rather reluctant *Rallié* defeated in the 1893 elections. De Poncheville recognized the need for an explicit adherence to the Republic by the delegates of the Congress. In his letter of invitation of
October 20 to Lamy he wrote,

Judging from the first meeting of the central committee held yesterday, there will be no difficulty in getting the Congress to adhere to the
Republic, but this adherence must be definitive and clearly formulated.
It will be a difficult task to organize French Catholics into a political
force and reach agreement with all the decent political elements in
the country.[49]

Because he did not approve of the Congress, Lamy did not go
to Rheims. He expressed his opinion of the gathering in a letter
written to Cardinal Rampolla on October 31, 1896.

This Congress was organized by men of good works. The choice of
presiding officers, all designated in advance, revealed its attitude. All
the officers were highly qualified in terms of their religious sentiments.
Some felt that Catholics should merely present themselves as Catholic
candidates. Others were Royalists. The only delegates who accepted
the Republic were those who broke with their political past in obedience to the Pope but who have little influence. The majority of the
delegates were hostile or indifferent to the *Ralliement*. None were
dedicated Republicans. All this would have little significance if the
Congress had devoted itself to charitable projects. Unfortunately its
leaders announced that it would consider political problems as well.
It is easy to see that the Congress of Rheims gave reactionary Catholics
the opportunity to appear as the initiators of Catholic activity.[50]

If the Congress of Lyons accepted the principle of the Republic
without accepting Republicans, the Congress of Rheims showed
that there were also many Catholics who were not even willing
to go that far. By the end of 1896 it had become apparent to Lamy
that he would need help if he were going to succeed in creating
a Catholic force that would submit to the will of the Vatican.
He felt that the movement might gain some momentum if a

[49] Lamy papers.
[50] *Cahier*, Lamy papers.

second Declaration endorsing his own Liberal Catholic views were issued by the five Cardinals. In the letter to Cardinal Rampolla cited above Lamy suggested that such a declaration might be supplemented by a speech delivered by himself tying the Cardinals' statement in with the various statements of the Vatican on the subject of the *Ralliement,* thereby adding both continuity and clarity to the movement.

In November 1896 Lamy contacted Cardinal Perraud, Bishop of Autun, and Cardinal Langénieux, Archbishop of Rheims. It had been Perraud who had originally suggested to Lamy the idea of the Declaration. It was hoped that Langénieux, the dean of the French Cardinals, would use his influence on behalf of the declaration. It is possible that Lamy thought that a statement from the Archbishop of Rheims endorsing his views would do much to offset the impression made by the Congress recently held in his city. Both Cardinals raised objections. In a letter to Lamy written on November 30, 1896, Perraud maintained that he still favored the issuing of a statement, but he was not sure that the grievances of the Church should be vindicated in terms of equal rights.[51] Langénieux felt that the clergy could not advocate the Liberal Catholic thesis even if some of its members privately agreed with it. As he wrote to Lamy on December 6, 1896, "Bishops can not suggest a line of conduct which in any way compromises doctrinal integrity. In so doing they would compromise the teachings of the Church . . ."[52] The refusal of these two influential clerics to compromise ecclesiastical doctrine as a concession to the existing situation ended the possibility of a second "Declaration of the Five Cardinals."

For Étienne Lamy 1896 was a year of probing and preparation. He had, it is true, succeeded in getting most Catholics to agree to the idea of unity. He could count on the fact that all but one Catholic group—that which had organized the Congress of

[51] A copy of this letter appears in the *Cahier,* Lamy papers.
[52] Lamy papers.

Rheims—adhered to the Republic. By the end of the year, however, it was readily apparent that he would run into difficulty as soon as he tried to impose his liberal principles on the majority of French Catholics.

Nevertheless in 1897 Lamy made further efforts to realize an effective political organization. One of his primary concerns as the elections of 1898 drew near was to coordinate the Catholic press. On April 18, 1897, he held a meeting which was attended by Eugène Veuillot of *L'Univers,* the Abbé Adéodat representing *La Croix,* and the Abbé Garnier representing *Peuple Français,* the mouthpiece of the *Union nationale.* Also present was Henri Lorin, representing *Le Petit Moniteur* and *La Politique Nouvelle,* which reflected the Catholic Republican position. It was agreed by all present that Catholic grievances should be expressed in terms of Republican principles. At a second meeting of the Catholic press Lamy was able to persuade the editors that Catholics had to look for support from other political elements.[53] Such harmony of opinion seems strange considering the reluctance of many Catholics to have anything to do with Republicans or Republican ideals. It should be remembered, however, that French Catholics, forced to rely upon themselves since 1893, were anxious to band together. This was as true for the Rheims group as it was for Lamy. Most Catholics either reluctantly or enthusiastically accepted the policy of the *Ralliement.* Thus all those present at the meetings at Lamy's house in April 1897 could agree in good conscience on the need for an improvement in the conditions of the Church. They could also agree on the need for associating with those who governed the Third Republic. However, the Abbé Adéodat and *La Croix* would lay emphasis on Catholic grievances rather than on the spirit of liberty, equality, and fraternity, and while the Abbé Garnier might accept the

[53] Copy of letter from Lamy to Rampolla, April 19, 1897, *Cahier,* Lamy papers. This letter contains three appendixes. The first describes the various meetings held by Lamy in April 1897.

idea of cooperating with the Opportunists, the concessions he might demand would probably be harsh enough to preclude any such cooperation.

On April 5, 1897, the first meeting of what later was to become known as the *Fédération électorale* took place at Lamy's house. Present at this meeting were the Comtes de Nicolay and De Bellemayre, representing the conservative Rheims group, Léon Harmel for the Christian Democrats, Boissard for *Justice-Égalité,* Bouvattier for the *Union nationale,* and Gaston David and Henri Lorin for the Catholic Republicans. These delegates were all laymen in conformance with Lamy's wish to exclude the clergy from active participation in political organizations.

At this meeting it was unanimously agreed to create a solid alliance between groups. It was to be left to each group to find its own formula for expressing its obedience to the wishes of the Vatican and to choose its means of action. This freedom of expression did not mean that any group could equivocate in its allegiance to the republican form of government.

It was also recognized unanimously that the purpose of the *Fédération* was to prepare a common program and a common list of candidates for the elections of 1898.

The more practical aspects of the organization were then discussed. It was agreed that each group would be invited by its delegates to submit to the *Fédération* complete information concerning its organization, its influence, its growth potential, its propaganda methods, and finally the strength of hostile political organizations. Once in possession of this information, the *Fédération* could coordinate it, and then draw up an electoral map of France in order to have a better idea of what had to be done and what role each group would play in the common cause.[54]

This report clearly reveals the ambiguities inherent in the *Fédération*. Given the differences of opinion within the organization as to the meaning of the *Ralliement,* the problem was how to find the proper balance between group autonomy and the

[54] Minutes of the meeting of April 5, 1897 in Gaston David's handwriting, Lamy papers.

central control which was essential to the success of the movement.

This problem continued to assert itself as the year 1897 ad-
vanced. In April the Méline ministry completed its first year in
office. Although it had the support of the Conservatives in the
Chamber, it had made no effort to change the laic laws. But it
was tolerant in its application of these laws. For example, it did
not force priests out of primary schools where there were no
ready replacements. Nonauthorized orders, including the Jesuits,
flourished. In short, the ministry tried to abide by the principles
of the *"esprit nouveau."* For French Catholics the question was
whether this tolerant attitude was sufficient, or whether the
ministry should be goaded into changing the hated laws.

Many Catholic Republicans favored cooperation with Méline.
They felt that the French political structure was rapidly evolving
into a two-party system. As one Catholic Republican, Paul Colombier, wrote to Lamy on April 26, 1897, "I assure you that the
situation is very different from what it was a few years ago.
There is a definite scission between the Radicals and the Opportunists. The break is not yet complete. There are still those who
would like to return to 'concentration,' but it becomes increasingly obvious that this is impossible, and when the break is
complete, the Opportunists will have to accept Catholic support." [55] Men like Colombier thought that in order to hasten and
encourage this break, Catholics should not embarrass the Opportunists by making excessive demands on the ministry. "Election
time is here again," wrote Fernand Laudet to Étienne Lamy from
the Gers on November 12, 1897:

Political reunions are being held in this department, important questions are being raised, and the press is agitating. Don't you think that
it would be a good idea if the *Politique Nouvelle* said something

---

[55] Lamy papers. Paul Colombier was an intimate friend of Lamy and it was to
him that Lamy willed his papers. Colombier's daughter married M. Dominique
Audollent who now owns the collection.

specific about the *lois scolaries et militaires* as soon as possible? Of course we don't approve of them, but isn't there a way of making this clear without appearing too inflexible, thereby frightening off the timid souls among the Opportunists and assuring the success of the Freemasons?

Should we not limit ourselves to combatting the atheistic and sectarian spirit which is responsible for these laws?[56]

In some departments even priests hoped that Catholic candidates would not be too categorical on the question of the laic legislation,[57] and in Digne (Basses-Alpes) it was reported that some Catholics did not want the local *La Croix* to support their candidate, Boni de Castellane, who had recently married the American heiress, Anna Gould, because such support might arouse anticlerical sentiment.[58]

As in the campaign of 1893, some Catholics felt that the crux of the matter was not the Catholic candidate but the Opportunist candidate whom Catholics could support. In some cases Catholics went so far as to hope that the Opportunist might not be forced to say anything that might compromise his Republican ideals. One wrote to Lamy, "In my opinion they [the Opportunist candidates] should limit themselves to general statements guaranteeing liberty and equality to Catholics rather than advocating specific changes in the anticlerical legislation."[59]

If there were Catholics who were urging a patient and conciliatory attitude toward the Méline ministry, others were considerably less inclined to compromise. The Rheims group and the Assumptionists took a hard line in their attitude toward the ministry. The former was still equivocating in its acceptance of the Republic. Lamy had persuaded the new papal nuncio, Monsignor Clari, to use his influence on the group to bring it

[56] Lamy papers.
[57] See letter from Victor Gay to Lamy, November 24, 1897, Lamy papers.
[58] See letter from Boissard to Lamy, October 26, 1897, Lamy papers.
[59] See letter from a Catholic in Lille (signature illegible) to Lamy, September 18, 1897, Lamy papers.

around, but the best the Nuncio could do was to get the group to
subscribe to the following formula: "The Rheims group accepts
the existing institutions of government, but it respects the private
convictions of its members." [60]

Equally annoying to Lamy was the attitude of the Assumptionists. He complained to the papal Secretary of State that
immediately after the first meeting of the *Fédération,* the *Justice-Égalité* committees had suspended their activity. The reason for
this was that both Lamy and the Vatican disapproved of overt
clerical involvement in politics. Since these committees were
usually headed by clerics, the Abbé Picard obediently removed the
priests from the committees, which he offered either to dissolve
or to place under the direct control of Lamy. This put the political
leader of the *Ralliement* in a difficult position. He refused to
allow clerical involvement, but at the same time he realized that
the *Justice-Égalité* committees without the priests were useless.

It is true that clerical activity in politics provokes Republican prejudices which are dangerous. It is also true that priests, and particularly
"the Fathers of *La Croix,*" are the only ones who have any influence
on the more ardent Catholics . . . This influence can not be passed on
to laymen. The only solution, therefore, is for the clergy to continue
providing inspiration for the *Justice-Égalité* committees while staying
behind the scenes. It should appear to the public as if these committees
were composed of and run by laymen.[61]

This was an interesting admission. Lamy was saying, in effect,
that he could not do without the Assumptionists because their
power and influence were far greater than his own.

Lamy further complained of the lack of centralization of the
Assumptionist organizations. It was impossible for the *Fédération*
to bring into line the various local organizations of the Assumptionists unless there was some sort of centralized authority.
Without this, there was no way of preventing a local *Justice-*

[60] See second appendix to letter from Lamy to Cardinal Rampolla, April 19,
1897, *Cahier,* Lamy papers.
[61] Third appendix, *ibid*. This appendix dealt with Lamy's difficulties with the
Assumptionists.

Égalité group from supporting a Royalist. This was because many Royalists posed as staunch Catholics. These Intransigents were in many cases attached to the *Fédération* through the Rheims group. Thus the Assumptionists, in supporting thoroughly "Catholic" candidates, were often supporting the anti-Republican cause. It was imperative that the order coordinate its activities and at the same time subordinate them to the wishes of Lamy. Here was another fundamental conflict between the Assumptionists and Lamy. It was in the formers' interest to allow for considerable autonomy on the local level, whereas it was in the latter's interest to coordinate and centralize all Catholic activity under himself.

Lamy was also disturbed by the activity of the Christian Democrats, particularly the Abbé Gayraud, who had scored such a triumph at the polls in Brest in the beginning of 1897. While it was a victory for a Catholic who accepted the Republic over one who did not, it was also a victory for the strongly clerical position. Lamy wrote of this to Cardinal Perraud in a letter dated March 8, 1897.

Universal suffrage no longer fears Catholic hostility to the Republic. It is anxious to achieve religious appeasement. At the same time it abhors a government of priests. The sudden, noisy agitation of priests and of the Catholic press has awakened this fear which it has been the object of the Vatican to dispel. The Brest election has shown what clerical influence can do to a clerical candidate. It gave the enemies of the Church an excellent opportunity to take up their cudgels again.[62]

Lamy had failed at the end of 1896 to get the help of the five cardinals in order to bring about Catholic unity under his aegis. In April 1897 the situation looked so unpromising that he decided to appeal to a higher level for help. He asked Cardinal Rampolla for support in bringing the Rheims group and the Assumptionists into line,[63] but the Vatican was reluctant to in-

[62] *Cahier,* Lamy papers.
[63] See copy of letter from Lamy to Rampolla, April 19, 1897, *Cahier,* Lamy papers.

tervene in an internal political situation in France for fear of violating the Concordat. The Pope was impressed by the recrudescence of Catholic activity since 1893, and he did not want to dampen this enthusiasm unless it was absolutely necessary. It was for this reason that Rampolla had urged respect for the autonomy of the various groups in his letter to Lamy of March 10, 1896.[64] Furthermore the Pope must have recognized, as did Lamy, that *La Croix* and *Justice-Égalité* were highly influential in Catholic circles. Monsignor Mourey, the Auditor of the Rota, wrote Lamy on December 10, 1897 that the Abbé Picard had considerable influence on Leo XIII because the head of the Assumptionists insisted that only his order could rally the hesitant Intransigents to the Republic.[65]

By the summer of 1897 Leo XIII realized that he would have to come to Lamy's support. In August he summoned two members of the French clergy to Rome: the Abbé Picard and Dom Sébastien Wyart, a former captain in the papal Zouaves, an ardent Vendéen Royalist, and at that time head of the Reformed Cistercian order in France. The Pope's idea was to send two distinguished clergymen, both known for their innate hostility to appeasement, on a tour of France to see to it that the clergy adhered to Vatican policy. By sending Wyart and Picard rather than two priests more sympathetic to conciliation, Leo XIII hoped to make their mission more compelling. The fact that the Abbé Picard was one of the so-called *missi dominici* might make it seem as if the Assumptionists as a whole had entirely submitted to the will of the Vatican. The precise instructions of the emissaries were sent out to each of them in letters from the Pope:

We have called you to Rome to undertake a mission of the utmost importance because of the situation in France, whom we love as the eldest daughter of the Church.

You are to go, in Our name, to the bishops of France and persuade

[64] Lamy papers.
[65] *Ibid.*

them that it is necessary that everyone strive to put an end to those unfortunate divisions, which afflict Us so profoundly, by uniting all decent men.

It is to be hoped that Our venerable brothers, the bishops, will in turn persuade influential men to put the good of their country above personal desires, however legitimate, by working energetically for the policy which We have laid down.

Your position at the head of a great monastic order will enable you to exert a powerful influence. Go then, in Our name, and overcome all prejudices and fears. Use every means in your power to convince the bishops that it is their bounden duty to put an end to the [religious] crisis.[66]

In practical political terms this meant that the *missi dominici* were to urge the bishops to support only those "Catholic" candidates who were fairly certain of success. Otherwise they were to support Méline's candidates.[67] These instructions were similar to those sent out by Lamy in the previous year, except that in the Vatican's instructions there was no mention of concessions to be exacted from the Opportunist candidates.

So anxious was the Vatican not to run into difficulty with the French government that the mission of Picard and Wyart was a secret even to Lamy, who got wind of it through his friend Monsignor Mourey.[68] The emissaries returned to Rome at the end of October 1897. They reported that they had been well received by the French episcopate but less well by the members of the lower clergy with whom they had come into contact. They gathered that Lamy had earned a reputation for not being Catholic enough and for being too involved in Republican politics. At the same time they received the impression that the *Justice-Égalité* committees were doing a good job.[69] Thus, in effect, Picard and Wyart did nothing to further the interests of Lamy, and from what is known of their mission, it is obvious

[66] Quoted in Louis Fichaux, *Dom Sébastien Wyart* (Lille, 1910), p. 624.
[67] See letter from Mourey to Lamy, September 18, 1897, Lamy papers.
[68] *Ibid.*
[69] Fichaux, *Dom Sébastien Wyart*, p. 636.

that they also did nothing to discourage the activities of the Assumptionists.

3

In December 1897 a second National Catholic Congress sponsored by the Rheims group was held in Paris. The Congress was attended by all elements of French Catholicism including the Catholic Republicans, who were represented by Jules Bonjean. Because he did not want to be overtly associated with any Catholic gathering, Lamy again did not attend. In fact, he had been opposed to the idea of the Congress because it was held under the auspices of the Rheims group and not the *Fédération*. "The attitude of this group toward the Republic is such that a congress sponsored by it would do nothing to promote the *Ralliement*. Paris would appear to be abandoning its monarchist sympathies only to replace them with another *Union de la France chrétienne*." [70] He had hoped that the Vatican would be able to use its influence to avoid such a congress. The fact that it was held and was sponsored by the Rheims group shortly after the mission of the *missi dominici* was a further indication that neither Lamy nor the Vatican was making much progress with a policy of conciliation.

The Congress of Paris was held between November 30 and December 5, 1897, and it was presided over by Thellier de Poncheville. As usual there were many speeches attacking the Freemasons, which were really attacks on the Third Republic. The Congress concluded with the announcement of the formation of the *Fédération électorale* which had actually been in existence since April 1897 but not publicized. The *Fédération* consisted of seven organizations. The Rheims group, the Catholic Republicans (known as the *Politique Nouvelle* group), the Christian Democrats, *Justice-Égalité,* and the *Union nationale* had all been previously associated with the *Fédération*. These

---

[70] Second appendix, letter from Lamy to Rampolla, April 19, 1897, *Cahier,* Lamy papers.

were joined in December by the *Action catholique de la jeunesse française* and the *Association catholique du commerce et de l'industrie,* two organizations primarily concerned with charitable works. It was announced publicly that Étienne Lamy was the president of the organization which adopted the following program: loyal acceptance of the constitution (*acceptation loyale du terrain constitutionnel*); reform of all laws not compatible with the principles of liberty and equality; and finally, cooperation with all political groups willing to support a just and fair government.[71]

The *Fédération* had accepted the basic principles laid down by Lamy in 1896. Catholic grievances were to be phrased in terms of Republican rather than Catholic ideals. It recognized the need to cooperate with Republican groups. More important than this, however, was the fact that the attitude of the *Fédération* as a whole toward adherence to the Republic was unsatisfactory from Lamy's point of view. The formula adopted by the Congress was not even close to that uttered by Cardinal Lavigerie (*adhésion sans arrière-pensée*) in his toast at Algiers. Since the program of the *Fédération* undertook to reflect the sentiments of all French Catholics, public opinion might well have concluded that the *Ralliement* had made little progress in seven years. The program appears to have been a compromise between Lamy's followers and more conservative Catholic elements. Lamy had succeeded in getting a statement accepting the principles of liberty and equality as well as recognition of the necessity to cooperate with other political elements. The conservative groups had succeeded in obtaining not only a vague statement accepting existing institutions but also an appeal for a reform of the laic laws which was bound to antagonize the Opportunists.

If Lamy was to succeed in convincing Méline's government that the *Fédération* supported the conciliatory approach of the Vatican, he had to be sure that the various Catholic groups with-

---

[71] *Compte rendu du congrès national catholique, 1897* (Paris, 1897), p. 460.

in the *Fédération* were cooperating with him. Even though there were strong differences of opinion among the groups, Lamy was able to obtain a general agreement to the effect that all political activity would be coordinated. This agreement was based upon three propositions: that the central committee of the *Fédération* was to be the final arbiter in the case of a conflict between two Catholic candidates in a given constituency; that candidates endorsed by the central committee were to be supported by all seven groups; and finally, that campaign funds were to be regulated by the central committee.[72]

Despite the fact that the Assumptionists had adhered to the above propositions, in actual practice they did not abide by them. The Auditor of the Rota complained to Lamy in a letter dated February 1, 1898, "The Assumptionists are the major obstacle to an agreement on candidates between you and the Opportunists."[73] During the campaign ". . . the Assumptionists in a number of instances supported candidates . . . who were not endorsed by the *Fédération*. They also made inopportune arrangements with other candidates. Their election funds were never properly amalgamated with the *Fédération* funds, and in some cases they sent money to candidates in their own name."[74]

As the elections drew closer the leader of the *Ralliement* realized that he would have to take a stand on the laic laws. Many of his supporters had been urging him for some time to avoid rigidity on this point, and it will be remembered that in 1892 the *Ligue pour la revendication des libertés publiques* had not pressed for immediate reform of these laws. Lamy wanted to cooperate with Méline. He knew that if too much were asked of the Premier it might do more harm than good. On the other hand, Méline had made no effort to change the laws. He had

[72] See letter from Lamy to Maurey, June 8, 1898; see also minutes of a meeting of the *Fédération électorale* on June 16, 1898 in Gaston David's handwriting, Lamy papers.
[73] Lamy papers.
[74] Lamy to Mourey, June 8, 1898, Lamy papers.

secured the support of Catholics and Conservatives by threatening them with the "Socialist menace." Lamy was well aware of this and warned Catholics not to let this tactic divert them from their main objective. He talked of a "policy which gets results." [75] In terms of political realities what did he take this to mean?

Lamy's opinion on this matter was to a large extent influenced by the Holy See. It had always been felt in Rome that a change in the laic laws could not be achieved until a general atmosphere of conciliation had been established. Before the elections of 1893 Leo XIII had insisted that *Rallié* candidates demand only minimum concessions, and he had not altered this position as the elections of 1898 approached. Realizing that there would be few *Fédération* candidates and many Opportunists running in Catholic areas, the Vatican stressed the importance of not asking too much of these Republicans. It was hoped that Opportunists would mention in their *professions de foi* that they respected the *"esprit nouveau"* without going into the question of the laic legislation. At the same time it was hoped that the ministry would at least remain neutral with regard to *Rallié* candidates. In a letter to Lamy dated November 19, 1897 Mgr. Mourey quoted Cardinal Rampolla as saying, "We ask only one thing and that is that the Opportunists do not refer to the laic laws as intangible." [76]

Lamy indicated his agreement with this approach in a letter written to Mgr. Mourey on November 19, 1897. [77] A simple statement supporting appeasement from Opportunist candidates and prefectoral neutrality with regard to *Fédération* candidates were set as minimum demands. More might be asked if the situation in a particular area warranted it. The president of the *Fédération électorale* revealed his negotiating principles in a letter which he wrote on March 16, 1898 to the Abbé Rembrand,

[75] Lamy to Jacques Piou, June 27, 1898, *Cahier,* Lamy papers.
[76] See letters from Mourey to Lamy of November 19 and November 24, 1897, Lamy papers.
[77] Lamy papers.

a prospective *Fédération* candidate in the Lot-et-Garonne. He mentioned the possibility of a second ballot in which the Opportunist in question would be opposed only by a Radical.

> In that case you will have to reach a specific agreement which will not embarrass M. Arago [the Opportunist candidate] and cause the more timid among his supporters to back M. Meillet [the Radical]. It is up to you to decide what is essential and what is not in framing the demands you will make of M. Arago. You must follow a policy which gets results. If you make the conditions for your support too inflexible, you might seriously jeopardize our cause. As of this moment M. Meillet is ahead, and you must realize that a number of Arago's supporters will abandon him if there appears to be a hint of clericalism.[78]

Lamy was unable to obtain Assumptionist cooperation on the crucial question of the laic laws, which he desperately needed in order to convince the Opportunists that French Catholics wanted conciliation. Neither he nor the Vatican could persuade the Assumptionists that an intransigent position on the laws would damage rather than help the cause of the Church. The "Fathers of *La Croix*" could not admit that a ministry which did nothing to change the hated laws should be supported. "I saw M. Lamy before I left Paris," wrote the Abbé Picard to the Abbé Bailly, editor-in-chief of *La Croix,* on November 4, 1897. "He is still trying to come to some kind of agreement with the ministry. If he succeeds it will be a good thing, but I feel that Lamy is too restrained in his demands when he should be asking for a great deal." [79] Furthermore, the Assumptionists were convinced, and quite rightly so, that their organizations were the most influential among those that made up the *Fédération* and that they and not Lamy should determine Catholic policy toward the elections. Picard spoke disparagingly of Lamy in another letter to Bailly.

> His influence appears to be negligible. In a meeting of various agents working in the departments which was held this morning, I was able

---

[78] Lamy papers.
[79] Quoted in Jarry, "L'Orientation politique," p. 1052.

to ascertain that in many of the departments Lamy's name is unknown. I was told that it was through the *Justice-Égalité* committees and *La Croix* that the provinces received information about the *Fédération* which still remains more of a myth than a reality.[80]

The attitude of the Rheims group was even less encouraging to Lamy. Émile Keller, one of the group's most distinguished members, wrote toward the end of 1897 that any attempt on the part of a Catholic to cooperate with a Republican ministry was tantamount to capitulation. He warned, "If there are any Catholics who are inclined to buy their election at the cost of giving in on the anticlerical legislation, one can only hope that they will get what they deserve. Better one more Radical than a cowardly Catholic."[81] Thellier de Poncheville, president of the Rheims group, in a speech on January 23, 1898, insisted that the purpose of the *Fédération* was to obtain from the government some kind of promise that the laic laws would be substantially modified.[82]

On April 18, 1898, less than a month before the elections, the *Fédération électorale* held a rally in the Salle Wagram in Paris. The main speaker was Étienne Lamy, who was making his first public appearance as the political leader of the *Ralliement*. His speech made no mention of cooperation with the Opportunists or of the minimum demands to be made of Opportunist candidates which both he and the Vatican favored. Instead it accused the government of not consistently pursuing a policy of appeasement.[83] What were the reasons for this rather hostile attitude on the part of Lamy? Had he decided at the last minute to adopt the Assumptionist approach? Lamy's actions during the elections would indicate that he had not abandoned his policy of compromise and cooperation. The most plausible reason for the tone

[80] Quoted in *ibid.*, p. 1053.
[81] Émile Keller, *Les Élections de 1898* (Paris, 1897), p. 12.
[82] Charles Thellier de Poncheville, *Droits et devoirs des catholiques* (Châlons-sur-Marne, 1898), p. 3.
[83] Étienne Lamy, *Les catholiques et la situation présente* (Paris, 1898), p. 1.

of the speech in the Salle Wagram was that Lamy as president of the *Fédération* was forced to emphasize grievances rather than appeasement at the rally in deference to the wishes of the more influential elements in that organization. In any event, the speech could hardly have been encouraging to Méline and his supporters.

The tensions and divisions within the *Fédération électorale* made the outcome of the elections a foregone conclusion. It is difficult to say how many candidates the *Fédération* ran in the elections of 1898. *La Politique Nouvelle* and *Le Petit Moniteur* referred to their candidates as Government Republicans, along with the Opportunists. So did *Le Figaro* and *L'Univers*. *La Croix,* on the other hand, often classified Royalists and Bonapartists as *Fédération* candidates. Henri Avenel, a reliable source, claimed that there were a hundred *Rallié* candidates in 1898 as opposed to ninety-four in 1893.[84] Since the major concern of Lamy had been to establish conditions for supporting Opportunists, it can safely be assumed that there were relatively few *Rallié* candidates.

The situation in the Haute-Garonne is one of the outstanding examples of how badly split French Catholics were in the elections of 1898. In this department there were several constituencies where the relationship between the Catholics and the Opportunists reflected the successes and the shortcomings of the *Ralliement*. In St.-Gaudens the ministry agreed to support the *Fédération candidate,* who in this case happened to be Jacques Piou, and in the third district of Toulouse the *Fédération* agreed to support the Opportunist, Creppi, who made no commitments other than a statement to the effect that he favored the *"esprit nouveau."*[85] The problem arose in the *arrondissement* of Villefranche. Here the *Fédération* had the choice of supporting either

[84] Henri Avenel, *Le Nouveau ministère et la nouvelle chambre* (Paris, 1898), p. 186.

[85] See letter from G. de Belemayre to Lamy, April 22, 1898. There are several letters from De Belemayre and others in the Lamy papers which give a detailed account of the electoral situation in the Haute-Garonne in 1898.

an Opportunist or a thinly disguised Bonapartist of the De Cassagnac variety. The leader of the *Fédération* in the Haute-
Garonne was a former Royalist, De Bellemayre. He was one of
the leaders of the Rheims group, and therefore was not kindly
disposed toward Republicans of any kind. The Opportunist candidate in Villefranche, a man by the name of Brocqua, refused
to go beyond a statement in favor of appeasement. For this reason De Bellemayre and *La Croix* refused to support him, con-
tending that Lamy's speech in the Salle Wagram had called for
Catholic support of only those Opportunists who favored a modification of the laic laws.[86] There were, however, other members
of the Haute-Garonne *Fédération* committee who were anxious
to support Brocqua, who was popular with most Catholics in the
region. Brocqua's supporters in the *Fédération* appealed to Lamy,
who endorsed the Opportunist. He was entitled to do this under
the agreement between the seven groups, which stated that in
the case of a conflict between candidates, the central committee
in Paris would be the arbiter. But Lamy sent the telegram con-
taining his instructions to De Bellemayre, who never revealed it
to the local committee. He and *La Croix* were able to exert
enough pressure on the *Fédération* so that Boutié, the Bonapartist, became the *Fédération* candidate. The result was that Villefranche was won by a Radical. In the constituencies where the
Opportunists cooperated, St.-Gaudens and the third district of
Toulouse, Piou and Creppi triumphed over Radical opposition.[87]
The same sort of situation existed in Bordeaux, where Catholics
found themselves at odds on the question of whether to support
Opportunists who would not agree to a change in the laic laws.[88]
A particularly striking example of the fatal division among
Catholics was provided by the department of the Gers in the

[86] De Bellemayre to Lamy, January 30, 1898, April 1, 1898, and April 22, 1898,
Lamy papers.
[87] See letter from A. Amillau, a supporter of Brocqua, to Lamy, June 15, 1898;
see also Constantin Manuel to Lamy, April 24, 1898, Lamy papers.
[88] See letter from E. Hourcade to Lamy, May 6, 1898, Lamy papers.

southwest. There the *Fédération* had agreed to support Fernand Laudet, a Catholic Republican and friend of Lamy, who was willing to postpone the burning question of reforming the laic laws. At a meeting of the departmental council on April 19, 1898, Paul de Cassagnac offered a resolution demanding the immediate abrogation of the *lois scolaires et militaires*. This was rejected by a large majority in the council including Laudet. The Assumptionist newspaper *La Croix de Gers* which was particularly influential in the department, consistent with its policy of supporting "Catholic" candidates wherever possible, decided on May 8 to give its support to the violently anti-Republican, De Cassagnac, thereby ignoring the decision of the *Fédération*. To illustrate how flexible the Assumptionists were in 1898, the *Croix du Nord* of May 5 gave its support to *Rallié* candidates who had made an agreement with the local Opportunists not to demand any kind of revision of the laic laws because there were no alternatives.

According to the Ministry of the Interior, whose figures were quoted in *L'Univers* of May 24, 1898, the *Ralliés* won approximately thirty-eight seats in the elections of May 8 and May 22, a slight gain over the number of seats won in 1893. The nucleus of their representation was formed by the Independent Republicans; this meant that although they had not been particularly staunch defenders of the rights of the Church during the sixth legislature, the *Fédération* was unable to replace them with more enthusiastic Catholic Republicans. For all the efforts of the Vatican and Étienne Lamy, the Church was largely represented in the new Chamber by either unenthusiastic Independent Republicans or by fire-eating anti-Republicans like Paul de Cassagnac. The Assumptionists, the Rheims group and many of the Christian Democrats gave the French electorate the impression that French Catholicism wanted to revive the ancient privileges of the Church—this despite the fact that there were other, less vociferous Catholic elements which supported Lamy and the Vatican.

The differences between those Catholics who favored appeasement and those who favored the "hard line" were profound. The Catholic Republicans, and to some extent the Christian Democrats, felt that French Catholicism had to come to terms with existing conditions and with the modern world. They realized that France was no longer a Catholic nation by belief and that the sooner the Catholic minority came to grips with this fact, the better their chances were of improving the situation. Their political approach was based upon a healthy respect for the art of the possible. The far more influential Assumptionists, on the other hand, refused to look reality in the face. France, they argued, had always been the eldest daughter of the Church. "They [the Assumptionists] loved battle too much. They fought only for their faith without the slightest thought of personal gain. They did not realize that in a nation which had undergone profound changes, the battle which they fought to restore traditional and antiquated forms of Catholicism to France was lost in advance." [89] The struggle within the *Fédération* was yet another example of the difficulty of the Catholic Church in adjusting to the principles of liberty and democracy.

On a more practical level there was another significant difference between Lamy and the Assumptionists which accounted for much of the latter's success among Catholics in 1898. Lamy believed that in order to bring all Catholic elements into line with his conciliatory policy, he would have to subject them to central control. This in spite of Denoyel's reports early in 1896 which indicated that local organizations resented outside interference. The Assumptionists were well aware of the prevalent desire for local political autonomy, and they founded the *Justice-Égalité* committees with this in mind.

[89] Jarry, "L'Orientation politique," p. 1059.

CHAPTER IV

The Opportunists and the Ralliement

 The Opportunists were the strongest of the three Republican groups in the Chamber of Deputies between 1890 and 1898, and their attitude toward the *Ralliement* was of crucial importance. The Radical position on the *Ralliement* never varied. The Catholic Church, whether it accepted the Republic or not, was, from their point of view, the enemy of modern society. For this reason there is little point in dwelling at length on the Radicals. It is necessary, however, to bear in mind the dilemma confronting this group between 1893 and 1898. The advent of a relatively large bloc of Socialists in the Chamber in 1893 put greater pressure on the Radicals from the left. They were not strong enough to stand on their own, and they badly needed allies. The question was whether they would unite with the Socialists to bring about social and economic reform or put pressure on the Opportunists to maintain "concentration."[1] This dilemma inevitably affected the politics of the Opportunists as well as the course of the *Ralliement*.

The Left-Centrists were a negligible force in the 1890's. Léon Say remained in the Chamber until his death in 1894, and Jules Simon continued to wield some influence through his articles in *Le Temps*. The organ of this group, however, was the *Journal des Débats,* a respected newspaper whose editorial opinion carried weight in a decade of conservative evolution.

[1] For the best discussion of Radical politics to date see Kayser, *Les Grandes batailles.*

The *Journal des Débats* (March 21, 1890) expressed the hope that the formation of Jacques Piou's *Droite constitutionnelle* in March 1890 was an indication that there would soon come into existence a responsible conservative party in response to the conservative sentiment that existed in the country. It argued in the edition of April 4, 1890 that anti-Republican Conservatives should be given every encouragement to rally to the Republic even though they could never be Republican in an orthodox way. The essence of the Left-Centrist view toward the *Ralliement* was contained in this statement:

We have often lamented the fact that there is no conservative party in the real sense of the term, but only a turbulent, agitating faction. We have always wanted a new party system based on alternative governmental programs rather than on destruction and revolution. We are happy to state that these ideas have been accepted by most conservatives including many clear-headed Monarchists.

But the Left-Centrists did not want to unite with the *Droite constitutionnelle,* even when that group finally accepted the Republic without reservation. "They [the *Ralliés*] should not be confused with the Liberal Republicans [the Left-Centrists] whose ideas we support and who wholeheartedly accept the program of the Liberal Union [the political organization of the Left-Centrists]. Resolute partisans of a policy of appeasement, intransigent adversaries of radicalism, our friends are more broad-minded on political questions and not as subject to religious influence as are the *Ralliés*. The Left-Centrists, for example, would never consider challenging the theory of secular education. They simply demand that this principle be applied in a spirit of conciliation with due respect for Catholic sentiments and beliefs."[2]

Convinced of the need for strong government to withstand the threat from the Left, these conservative Republicans had by 1893 abandoned the position of opposition which they had taken

[2] *Journal des Débats,* July 25, 1893.

in 1885. They called for a homogeneous majority made up of themselves and the Opportunists which would lay the foundation for a strong government.[3]

Between 1893 and 1898 the Left-Centrists supported all governments with the exception of the Radical Bourgeois ministry. They were particularly enthusiastic about the Méline ministry. By this time there was nothing to distinguish them from the Independent Republicans who were also calling for a strong government and who were coming to support Opportunist ministries to an increasing extent. The *Ralliement* had succeeded in reuniting the Left and Right Centrists who had broken from each other in 1875 over the constitutional question. In 1893, however, this could hardly be considered a momentous political event. The balance of power had shifted to the left, and it was not the Left-Center that the *Ralliés* had to convince but rather the Opportunists.

The Opportunists were loosely organized. Some, like Eugène Spuller, Jules Méline, and Joseph Reinach, had been closely associated with Gambetta in the 1870's, and others with Jules Ferry. The Opportunists almost always voted with the government. They were uniformly hostile to socialism or anything resembling it, and they were ardently Republican, accepting the laic laws as fundamental to the well-being of their country. What many Opportunists wanted, now that the Republic as they had conceived it had been firmly established, was to put an end to the constitutional quarrels of the 1870's and 1880's in order to focus on economic and social problems.

There were three phases in the development of the Opportunists' attitude toward the *Ralliement*. The first phase began with the liquidation of the Boulanger affair in 1890 and ended with the elections of 1893. The second began with the formation of the Jean Casimir-Perier ministry in 1893 and ended with the

---

[3] Declaration of the *Union libérale républicaine* in *Journal des Débats*, July 12, 1893.

fall of the Bourgeois ministry in April 1896. The final phase began with the formation of the Méline ministry in 1896 and ended with the fall of that ministry in June 1898.

In the elections of 1889 the *profession de foi* of Paul Deschanel, a bright young Opportunist candidate and future President of the Republic, reflected the sentiments of many of his group.

It is time for enlightened Conservatives worthy of the name to abandon factious politics and loyally accept the constitution. For twelve years I have been urging Conservatives in our department [Eure-et-Loire] to do this . . . I have explained to them that there is no salvation for them *or for us* except in the formation of a conservative party, a Tory party, within the Republic.[4]

Here was a Republican calling for the rallying of conservative forces to the Republic a year before the formation of the *Droite constitutionnelle* and the toast at Algiers. Although the Republicans had joined forces during the elections of 1889, there was a strong feeling on the part of many Opportunists dating back to 1885 that the Republic could be solidly established only when the anti-Republicanism of the Right had been overcome. Ernest Constans' negotiations with De Mackau after the collapse of Boulangism were an indication of this feeling.

There was considerable talk of appeasement among Opportunists between 1890 and 1893. The problem lay in deciding what it meant. Did appeasement mean that Republicans should reconsider the laic legislation or did it merely mean that these laws should be applied with tolerance? There were a number of ways in which a ministry could be tolerant without advocating a change in the laws. It could tacitly agree to the return of the many orders exiled since 1880. It could be flexible in its application of the *loi scolaire,* which meant that no pressure would be put on various communities which had not yet replaced the priests with lay teachers in the primary schools.

[4] Paul Deschanel, *Questions actuelles* (Paris, no date), p. 311. The italics are mine.

For all Opportunists the desire for appeasement had to be weighed against the fear of being accused by the Radicals of being un-republican. Could they continue to associate with the Radicals while they made overtures to the Right? This problem was implicit in a speech of Joseph Reinach on the seventh anniversary of Gambetta's death (quoted in *La République Française* of January 6, 1890).

My fellow citizens, we must rise above the petty religious and constitutional disputes which aid no one but the enemies of the Republic. Let us openly admit that we are against the spirit of factiousness and intolerance. We must retain the most effective of our weapons, that unity born of a serious menace to the Republic. At the same time we can not reject anyone who accepts the Republic loyally in order to serve the nation which has freely chosen that form of government.

The Opportunists were on the whole favorable to the formation of the *Droite constitutionnelle*. On March 22, 1890, Reinach stated in *La République Française* (a newspaper founded by Gambetta) that true Republicans should not prevent Conservatives from rallying to the Republic, especially at a time when France had to appear united. He pointed out that the Republicans in the National Assembly had not prevented the rallying of certain Orleanists in 1875 and that this served as adequate precedent. What was important, from Reinach's point of view, was that Piou and his followers indicate their loyalty to the Republic by acts as well as by words. But if Opportunist sentiment tended to endorse the rallying of the Right, it was not impressed by the vague and ambiguous statements of the *Droite constitutionnelle* in 1890. In an article published in *La République Française* on December 18, 1890, Eugène Spuller summed up this feeling:

We must observe that if M. Piou, while accepting the Republic, fails to inspire confidence in his political position, he will never acquire the strength he needs to be a strong influence among the Conservatives, and his evolution toward the Republic will be useless ...

In politics, the best, the easiest, and the most advantageous way to act is to act with a decisiveness that can inspire no doubts. This does not mean that one should not deliberate before resolving to act. It means that once a position is taken, it should be taken without doubts or equivocations.

The Opportunists received Cardinal Lavigerie's toast with considerably more enthusiasm than they had the formation of the Piou group. This was because the Cardinal had advocated the acceptance of the Republic without reservations. *Le Temps* of November 14, 1890, referred to the infinite wisdom of Lavigerie while reiterating the point made earlier that it would take time for his words to have an effect in Catholic and Conservative circles. In *La République Française* of November 16, 1890, Reinach deplored the hostile reception given by these circles to the toast in an editorial in which he presented the Cardinal and the Opportunists as guardians of the spirit of the Edict of Nantes, and the Radicals and Intransigents as the destroyers of that spirit.

The toast and Cardinal Rampolla's letter to the Bishop of St.-Flour caused some Opportunists to re-evaluate their views on religion. Jules Méline, in a speech at Remiremont in the Vosges which was published in *La République Française* of January 8, 1891, called religion a great moral and social force. Religion, he said, should not be destroyed; in fact the government should encourage religious activity. While admitting that he was a fervent partisan of the laic laws, he insisted that these laws had to be applied in a spirit of toleration.

There were other Opportunists who argued that if there were a real conciliation between Church and State, the Church would no longer be dependent on the Bonapartists and the Monarchists. Once it was free of its past associations, its moral and spiritual force might be counted on to counteract the danger from the left. "Thus we must not spurn a policy of appeasement," wrote Spuller. "No other policy is possible for our government, no other policy is possible for the Church."[5]

[5] Eugène Spuller, *L'Évolution politique et sociale de l'église* (Paris, 1893), p. 250.

Such sentiment received encouragement from Leo XIII's encyclical *Au milieu des sollicitudes*. Commenting on it, Spuller had this to say:

... The Pope wants appeasement and so does our government. Both are horrified by the coalition of extremist parties in the Chamber. France, above and beyond anything else, desires order and stability.

The era of religious quarrels is over. France has other problems. Her people want to work and live quietly.[6]

The Gouthe-Soulard crisis in 1891 was a blow to these optimistic hopes. *La République Française* of December 12, 1891 warned the French bishops who sided with the Archbishop of Aix-en-Provence that they were playing into the hands of the enemies of the Republic as they had done during the formative years of the Third Republic and during the Boulanger crisis. Complicity with the enemies of the Republic had never done anything to further the cause of the Church. Whenever the Republic was threatened, Republicans united in its defense— which invariably proved successful. Spuller commented in *La République Française* of December 13, 1891 that the activity of Archbishop Gouthe-Soulard and his sympathizers was a classic example of "clericalism," which he carefully distinguished from "religion."

We have heard much in the past few days of the slogan "*Le cléricalisme, voilà l'ennemie.*" Justification for the existence of this slogan continues to exist. Clericalism is not religion, nor should it necessarily be identified with the Catholic Church, which has too often been compromised by the enemies of the Republic. "*Cléricalisme*" means the intrusion of representatives of the Church in politics. Such intrusion can never be tolerated by the French nation, which is indissolubly linked to the Republic.

The Opportunists could not tolerate a threat to the Concordat, which was, from their point of view, the means by which the Church was manipulated and controlled. During the uproar

---

[6] Spuller, *L'Évolution politique*, p. 269.

instigated by the Archbishop of Aix there had been much talk among the Intransigents of the separation of church and state. Spuller and others were afraid that if the Catholics became too alienated, then separation was inevitable. Such fears served to increase the desire for appeasement on the part of many Opportunists.[7]

The Gouthe-Soulard crisis showed how acute the differences between the two major Republican groups had become despite their solidarity during the elections two years earlier. The Radicals were now provided with an excellent opportunity to insist once again on separation. *Le Temps* of November 26, 1891, lamented the fact that fanaticism on the Left was equally as harmful as that on the Right. "This clash of doctrines and contradictory fanaticisms will make it much more difficult to achieve that pacification which is the fervent desire of all reasonable men, laymen and clergy alike."

An excellent example of the different philosophies of the two groups is provided by the debate in the Chamber on January 29, 1891. The government, then headed by Freycinet, had censored a play by Sardou entitled *Thermidor* which had recently appeared on the stage of the *Comédie Française*. The play was critical of the Jacobin phase of the Revolution, although it lauded the revolutionary ideals of 1789. The government had censored it because Léon Bourgeois, the Minister of Education, felt that criticism of any part of the Revolution was criticism of the whole. The Opportunists found the ministry's action distasteful because in essence they agreed with the play. The Radicals defended the action because they could not bear any attack on the great Jacobin tradition. Joseph Reinach rose to defend the early phase of the Revolution.

There is no one in the Chamber who believes more profoundly in the French Revolution, who loves, honors, and respects it more, or who is more grateful to it than I. Because I honor and respect it

[7] *Ibid.*, p. 190.

as the cradle of modern France, I do not confuse the honest, incomparable patriots who gave liberty to France and to the world with men who for many months made the nation submit to the most terrifying and most odious of tyrannies.[8]

It was in this debate that Clemenceau uttered the remark, "Gentlemen, whether we like it or not, the French Revolution is a unit (*la révolution française est un bloc*) . . . One cannot accept one part of it and reject another." [9] This statement was, in effect, a challenge to the Republican orthodoxy of the Opportunists.

The Panama scandal did nothing to heal the breach. Despite the fact that it afforded the Intransigents an excellent opportunity to jeer at Republican corruption, it did not produce the instinctive union betwen the two groups as similar attacks had done in the past. This fact had so encouraged Jacques Piou that for the first time he began to think in terms of a possible alliance between his group and the Opportunists. The Radicals demanded that the government show more diligence in its investigations. A Radical proposition giving greater powers to a parliamentary investigating committee was opposed by many Opportunists on the grounds that it was an encroachment of the legislative upon the powers of the administration.[10] *Le Temps* of November 24, 1892, commented:

This story has a moral to it . . . It reveals the temerity of the Chamber, it reveals the kind of revolutionary measures the Chamber will adopt when it gets carried away in the heat of debate . . . It is time for the Chamber to get hold of itself and for the government to reestablish its ascendancy. Both are vital to the security of the country.

Developing this theme in *La République Française* of November 30, 1892, Spuller pointed out that a ministry which could not command a homogeneous majority did more harm than good.

[8] J. O., Chambre, *Débats* (January 29, 1891), p. 150.
[9] *Ibid.*, p. 156.
[10] *Ibid.* (November 26, 1892), pp. 565–583.

It would be wrong to imagine that all Opportunists were in favor of a total break with the Radicals. There was still a strong tendency on the part of both groups to adhere to the principle of "concentration." Raymond Poincaré, a rising figure among the Opportunists, recalled in an article which appeared in *La République Française* of February 24, 1892, that it had been "concentration" which had destroyed Boulangism. "We are resolved to do everything in our power to maintain a union which seems to us as necessary today at it was yesterday and which will prove to be necessary tomorrow." It was almost as if Poincaré, in 1892, was predicting the Dreyfus Affair.

For the Opportunists the difficulty was that they wanted to have their cake and eat it too. They wanted to maintain Republican unity, but on their terms. They wanted religious pacification and cooperation from the Right, but again on their terms. Could they remain the dominant force in the Third Republic as they had been since 1879 without making concessions to either the Left or Right? It was a difficult problem for the Opportunist leaders who appeared to be adopting different approaches to it as the elections of 1893 drew nearer. Charles Dupuy, whose ministry presided over the elections, delivered a ringing speech in Toulouse on May 21, 1893, in which he called for a union of all Republicans from the extreme Left to the Center. He called the *Rallié* candidates hypocrites because in his opinion they were secretly collaborating with the Royalists.[11] Two weeks later, however, Ernest Constans who in 1889 had been largely responsible for pricking the Boulangist balloon, made a speech in the same city, in which he stressed the need for order. The former Minister of the Interior stated that the time for defense of the Republic was over and that the period for organization had begun. By organization he meant the establishment of a strong government based on a homogeneous majority. Constans then brought up the question of the *Ralliement*. He welcomed those

[11] *La République Française*, May 22, 1893.

Conservatives who sincerely adhered to the Republic and suggested that this might be made easier for them if the government proved tolerant. Toleration did not mean a change in the laic laws.

> Let us not deceive ourselves, gentlemen. When a Republican speaks of religious peace, he is not asking for a revision of those laws which at the time they were passed caused considerable opposition to them. These laws are, in effect, accepted today even by those who in the past objected to them. No, it can never be a question of asking the Republic to retreat from a position previously taken. We must protect our patrimony in its entirety.[12]

Despite its uncompromising stand on the laic laws Constans' speech could be construed as encouraging to the *Ralliés*.

For the first time since 1879 there was almost no attempt to revive Republican unity during an electoral campaign, Dupuy's speech in Toulouse to the contrary. It seemed as if the days of the defense of the Republic were over, as Constans had said. The Radicals, although they were far from unified, were calling for political and social changes, and some were going so far as to call for a majority in the new Chamber composed of Radicals and Socialists.[13] The pressure for change from the Left made it impossible for many Opportunists to consider reviving the old union. The Panama crisis had made it clear to them that what was now needed was a government supported by a workable majority rather than a static one. Wrote Spuller in *La République Française* of August 18, 1893, "Elect men of government! Create a viable majority which will produce a firm, stable and enlightened government."

The Opportunist demand for ordered government corresponded exactly with the demands of the *Droite républicaine* and the Left-Centrists. Despite this identity of interests inspired by the growing fear of socialism among all elements of French conservatism, the Opportunists were not inclined to associate

---

[12] Quoted in *La République Française*, June 5, 1893.
[13] Kayser, *Les Grandes batailles*, pp. 198–204.

with the *Rallíés*. The tardy and reluctant acceptance of the Republic by the followers of Piou was to a large extent responsible for this. Furthermore, the aggressive attitude of many French Catholics including the Christian Democrats toward Republicans was not conducive to electoral alliances. "The *Rallíés* are men who belonged to anti-Republican parties whom the Church wishes to lead into battle today as it did yesterday. It is a change in tactics, but clericalism still exists." [14]

As the elections drew closer the tendency among the old associates of Gambetta and Ferry was to campaign for an exclusively Opportunist majority. Spuller, disillusioned by the seeming lack of enthusiasm among the supporters of Piou, wrote in *La République Française* of August 9, 1893, "Opportunism, which so many spit upon, distrust and despise, has achieved for France all that we have today. The Radicals have done nothing, even when they were in power, because they themselves, once in power, became Opportunists." In Draguignan, in the Var, the Opportunists campaigned against Clemenceau and were successful. In numerous other constituencies the two Republican groups opposed one another.[15] At the same time the Opportunists fought the *Rallíés*. Three quarters of the *Rallíé* candidates were opposed by Opportunists despite the efforts of the former to cooperate.

The Opportunists emerged from the elections with enough seats to support a ministry without help from either Right or Left. The Radicals had made some gains, but some of their most vociferous leaders—Clemenceau, Stephen Pichon, and Floquet—were defeated. The Socialists had also made impressive gains.[16] The Opportunists' appeal for appeasement had considerable effect on Conservative voters, who in many departments

---

[14] Eugène Spuller in *La République Française,* July 21, 1893.

[15] Kayser, *Les Grandes batailles,* pp. 203–204.

[16] *Le Temps,* September 5, 1893 and A. Daniel, *L'Année Politique,* 1893, list 311 Opportunists, 122 Radicals, 49 Socialists, and 25 *Rallíés*. Republicans of both groups picked up seats from the Right.

deserted Conservative candidates even though in some instances the Conservatives had rallied.[17] Jules Méline, newly appointed editor-in-chief of *La République Française,* saluted the triumph of his group at the polls in the edition of November 4, 1893 and added,

It is time to take a new road and to lay aside factious quarrels and religious disputes. We appeal to all men of good faith to work together to perfect the government and administration of the country . . .

We firmly believe that defense of our agriculture and industry, the life-blood of the nation, is the important issue at hand. The salvation of our country depends upon a successful defense.

It remained to be seen whether the Opportunists would be able to stand on their own or whether they were still subject to pressures from Right and Left.

2

In the debate in the Chamber on November 23, 1893, Paul Deschanel insisted that his group was indeed independent.

When there were two hundred Monarchists in the Chamber there was no other policy possible other than that of the union of the different Republican groups and the constitution of ministries in which each group was represented.

As the Republic became more solidly established, as the old dynastic parties disappeared, it was inevitable that each one of these groups became more independent, first in the elections, and then in the Chamber, and that each group tried to make its ideas prevail over those of others.[18]

The speaker listed the differences between the two major Republican groups on the issues at hand. Whereas the Radicals wanted to weaken the powers of the President of the Republic even further and to eliminate the Senate, the Opportunists wanted to keep these institutions intact. Although the Radicals wanted the

[17] Siegfried, *Tableau politique,* p. 466.
[18] Quoted in Paul Deschanel, *République nouvelle* (Paris, 1898), pp. 61–62.

progressive income tax, the Opportunists wanted to increase taxes on various types of revenue. The Radicals wanted to nationalize the railroads, and the Opportunists believed that there could be railroad reforms without nationalization. Finally, the Radicals wanted separation of church and state; the Opportunists, on the other hand, wished to maintain the Concordat. What was particularly significant in Deschanel's speech was the refusal to admit the inevitability of an alliance with the Right.

Three months after the elections the Dupuy ministry gave way to a ministry which reflected the new majority in the Chamber more precisely. This ministry, headed by Jean Casimir-Perier, was attractive to most conservative elements. Casimir-Perier's grandfather had been a minister under Louis-Philippe, and his father had played an important role in creating the *ordre morale* of the 1870's. The new Premier was well connected in the world of finance and industry and was extremely wealthy. At the same time he was a staunch Republican. In his ministerial statement he expressed greater concern for the threat from the Left than for the danger from the Right.

Gentlemen, the government which presents itself before you will devote its energies to obeying the will of the electorate as recently expressed. France has never stated with greater force her attachment to the Republic and her aversion to a reactionary regime. She has also expressed her respect for freedom of thought and of conscience, as well as for progress. Never has she more clearly condemned policies based on abstract formulas, arbitrary classifications and unjustified prejudices. In the face of these theories held by a certain school of thought, France emphatically demands the maintenance of order and the defense of those principles established by the French Revolution as the basis for modern society.[19]

The outstanding event of the Casimir-Perier ministry was the speech made by Eugène Spuller, Minister of Public Worship, calling for a "new spirit." The evocation of this principle during the debate in the Chamber on March 3, 1894, revealed nothing

[19] J. O., Chambre, *Débats* (December 4, 1893), p. 196.

new about the politics of the Opportunists. No concessions were made to the Right. The Premier himself rose to reiterate that the laic laws were a part of the nation's patrimony.[20] What was important about this declaration was that an Opportunist minister felt confident enough to make what was in essence an appeal to the Right without worrying about its effect on the Radicals. The question remains why such an appeal was necessary only a short time after the Opportunists' success in the elections.

The *"esprit nouveau"* statement indicated that many Opportunists were increasingly concerned about the Left. They were convinced that the structure of French politics was changing and that there would soon be a two-party system with the Opportunists and Conservatives allied against the Radicals and the Socialists. They hoped that the Conservatives, equally afraid of the Socialists, would rally to the Opportunist Republic, forgetting the grievances of the past. "We all need each other," said Eugène Spuller in *La République Française* on April 10, 1894. "That is why a policy of reconciliation, concord, and appeasement, of which I am an advocate, must be adopted by all men of peace and good will." The reference to men of good will was reminiscent of the language of Leo XIII. What the Opportunists wanted was a large and disciplined majority strong enough to govern the country on their terms. They had talked of this before the elections, but the need for it had become more apparent with the Socialists' success at the polls.

One of the leading advocates of a strong government was René Waldeck-Rousseau, who returned to the political arena early in 1895 after a decade of practicing law. Waldeck-Rousseau saw no need to apologize for being a conservative Republican. In a speech delivered at Roanne on November 15, 1895, he said, "To be a conservative Republican is to attach oneself completely to the ideals of the French Revolution in order to defend them

[20] J. O., Chambre, *Débats* (March 3, 1894), pp. 486–487.

from new attacks with the same ardor and the same determination with which we defended them against the counter-Revolution." [21] Reiterating the need for order in another speech at Montbrison (quoted in *L'Univers* of March 9, 1895), he said, "But now we must ask ourselves what measures we should take in order that this nation continue to thrive. At a time when economic and social questions dominate politics we must put an end to anarchy and abstract theories that can never be realized." How was this to be accomplished? By reviving true Republican unity, which had overcome the crises of May 16 and Boulangism. For Waldeck-Rousseau the defense of order and liberty was in itself an ideal which could inspire true Republicans to form a disciplined majority. Would this new union exclude the *Ralliés?*

The Republican party must remain faithful to its principles but at the same time it must be tolerant. If the Republic is fortunate enough to gather new adherents it should rejoice. If these adherents are not forthcoming, it is because there are too many people who say that anyone who calls himself a Republican must think as they do. I consider that the adherence to the Republic of a considerable element of French opinion which up until now has been isolated and subject to political discontent, and which up until now has been dangerous to the well-being of the country is one of the guarantees of the future.

It is to the conquest of those who have been dissatisfied with the Republic that we must devote our efforts. To do this we must have a government with the courage of its convictions which can act responsibly without having to consider the machinations of various groups in the Chamber.

The fear that the Opportunists were drifting too far to the Right brought about a reaction from the left wing of their majority not long after the elections of 1893. The Casimir-Perier ministry fell in May 1894 after a debate concerning the right of state railroad employees to form unions, and in which a large

---

[21] Quoted in René Waldeck-Rousseau, *Opinions de M. Waldeck-Rousseau* (Paris, 1902), pp. 4–5.

number of Opportunists either abstained or voted against the government. The subsequent Dupuy ministry, which included Louis Barthou and Raymond Poincaré, had difficulty with left-wing Opportunists led by Gustave Isambert and known as the *Union progressiste*.[22] Because they disliked losing contact with the Radicals, the chief aspiration of Isambert and his followers was to revive "concentration."[23] The group fluctuated in size depending upon the issue at hand, but it was influential enough to destroy the illusion of a homogeneous Opportunist majority. It was responsible for Brisson's victory over Méline as President of the Chamber in December 1894, and it was also responsible for the formation of the Ribot ministry in January 1895 which included two Radicals.[24] It was under this ministry that the crisis over the *droit d'abonnement* occurred.

The Ribot ministry sincerely believed that this tax was simply a readjustment of an old tax which had been difficult to collect. The fact remains, however, that the government insisted on the tax at a time when Catholics were particularly sensitive, and only a year after the appeal for a "new spirit." The Clausel de Coussergues amendment, referred to in the preceding chapter, which was acceptable not only to the *Ralliés* in the Chamber but to many Opportunists who believed that the amendment was a conciliatory gesture, was not entirely acceptable to Ribot, who refused to consider a reduction of the amount of the tax.[25] The ministry was undoubtedly making an effort to placate the Radicals.

The lack of unity among Opportunists was lamented by the leaders of those groups which had been optimistic about a homogeneous majority after the elections of 1893. Eugène Spuller wrote in *La Revue Politique et Parlementaire:*

[22] Goguel, *La Politique des partis*, p. 74.
[23] *Ibid.*, p. 73. See also A. Soulier, *L'Instabilité ministérielle sous la Troisième IIIe République* (Paris, 1939), p. 421.
[24] Soulier, *L'Instabilité ministérielle*, p. 421.
[25] *La République Française*, March 18, 1895.

We flattered ourselves in thinking that we had finished with the politics of "concentration" after the elections of 1893, and that on all sides there was a demand for a ministry supported by a disciplined majority . . . We had hoped that this majority would be open to all who were willing to cooperate with us in order to maintain the discipline essential to a stable ministry. Such a ministry was that of M. Casimir-Perier which was unable to last even six months. It was not the ministry which was at fault, however, but the constantly vacillating Opportunist majority riddled with internal divisions . . .[26]

A significant event during the period 1893–1896 was the resignation of Casimir-Perier as President of the Republic. Chosen in June 1894 to replace the assassinated President Sadi-Carnot, his election had been enthusiastically received in all conservative circles. Although the office was not endowed with much power other than the right to select a potential Premier, it was felt by some that because there was an Opportunist majority in the Chamber and because Casimir-Perier was a rising star in the political firmament, something might be done to readjust the balance between the executive and legislative branches of government. It was the first time in the history of the Third Republic that a strong personality had been elected President. The election produced a violent reaction from the Radicals, Socialists, and the *Union progressiste,* and every effort was made to discredit Casimir-Perier. In January 1895 the President of the Republic resigned. His letter of resignation addressed to the two chambers was another expression of the disillusionment felt by many Opportunists.

During the past six months there has been a campaign of defamation and vilification against the army, the magistrature, Parliament and the President of the Republic. Yet this right to stir up hatred and social discontent continues to be called freedom of thought . . .

Unalterably faithful to myself, I remain convinced that the reform we so badly need will not be carried out unless there is a government capable of assuring respect for the law, and which can be sure of

[26] Eugène Spuller, "Quatorze mois de la législature," *Revue Politique et Parlementaire,* 3:9 (January 1895).

the obedience of its supporters thereby directing their activity toward a common good.[27]

His language was similar to that later used by the Republican *anti-Dreyfusards*.

The Ribot ministry fell on October 28, 1895, and was replaced by one composed uniquely of Radicals headed by Léon Bourgeois. The new premier was one of those Radicals who feared an alliance with the Socialists and because of this was attracted to the idea of reviving "concentration." He had tried, unsuccessfully, to bring Opportunists into the ministry.[28] Bourgeois and Émile Combes, the new Minister of Public Worship, made no attempt to hasten the separation of church and state. The ministry's chief aim was to introduce the progressive income tax against the opposition of the Opportunists, Independent Republicans, Left-Centrists, and Intransigents.

Some Opportunists were actually encouraged by the existence of the Bourgeois ministry because they believed that its existence placed the Radicals in a difficult situation. Either the Radicals would be forced to conclude an alliance with the Socialists, in which case Opportunists such as Isambert would reject forever the idea of reviving "concentration," or they would repudiate the Socialists, in which case they would appear to betray their reform program, thereby losing considerable support in the country. In either case, it was felt that the position of the Opportunists would be strengthened.[29]

The Bourgeois ministry lasted a little more than five months. It had succeeded in passing the progressive income tax in the Chamber by seven votes, which indicated that there were a number of Opportunists who clung to the hope of "concentration" to such an extent that they were willing to allow the passage of a relatively radical economic reform. It took the more conservative Senate finally to topple the ministry on April 21, 1896.[30]

[27] Quoted in Daniel, *L'Année Politique,* 1895, pp. 9–10.
[28] Goguel, *La Politique des partis,* p. 74.
[29] Kayser, *Les Grandes batailles,* p. 233.
[30] Goguel, *La Politique des partis,* p. 75.

The Radical interlude of 1895–1896 was of the utmost importance to the political evolution of the 1890's. The income tax issue had aroused the anger of conservatives of every sort. It convinced the *Ralliés* in the Chamber once and for all that they would have to associate with the Opportunists at the cost of the laic laws. It caused the Intransigents to relax their hostility to *all* Republicans. But most of all, it served to widen the split among the Opportunists. Jules Méline, Paul Deschanel, Louis Barthou, Raymond Poincaré, and Waldeck-Rousseau were more than ever convinced of the need for a disciplined conservative Republican majority. Others, like Gustave Isambert, continued to worry about the implications of a conservative Republic and longed for the good old days of "concentration."

3

Félix Faure succeeded Casimir-Perier as President of the Republic in 1895. He was fully aware of the passions aroused among all Republicans during Bourgeois' tenure of office and instinctively returned to the idea of "concentration," summoning Sarrien to institute a Cabinet composed of the various Republican elements. When Sarrien failed, Faure then turned to Jules Méline.[31]

Méline, who was fifty-eight years old in 1896, had been a deputy from the Vosges since 1872 and had been closely associated with Gambetta and Spuller. In 1894 he had succeeded Joseph Reinach as editor of *La République Française,* the influential Opportunist newspaper. His chief interests were in economic problems, particularly those pertaining to agriculture, and he had been the leader of the protectionist forces which had in 1891 overcome the proponents of free trade. In this capacity he had been closely associated with many Conservatives who were attracted to protectionism because they were landowners.[32] Méline was well received by many Opportunists, by the Independents, and even by

[31] Daniel, *L'Année Politique,* 1896, pp. 159–160.
[32] Georges Lachapelle, *Le Ministère Méline* (Paris, 1928), chap. 1.

the Intransigents, because they saw in him a bulwark against Socialism.

Méline was certain that the political structure had undergone a considerable change with the decline of the "revolutionary" Right and the rise of the "revolutionary" Left and that the time had come for the institution of a two-party system. On January 21, 1895, he wrote in *Le République Française:*

Up until now the majority in the Chamber has not been consistent. It would be easy to solidify a majority if there were a government of action rather than inaction as was unfortunately the case under the second Dupuy ministry.

There can be no question about the fact that we are going to have two parties which will engage in a struggle for power and which will increase the bitterness which already exists in the Chamber. The magic word "concentration" can mean nothing in these times simply because ministries of this sort have achieved nothing. We must be realistic.

Despite the fact that he saw "concentration" as a thing of the past, Méline, when called upon to form a ministry, attempted to draw two Radicals into it. These men refused, leaving Méline free to form a solidly Opportunist cabinet. If the new Premier was persuaded that the Radicals were on their way to becoming solid allies of the Socialists and that the two-party system was almost a reality, what explains this attempt to revive an anachronism? The only satisfactory explanation is that the instinct for Republican unity was deeply embedded in all Republicans.

Méline's ministerial statement before the Chamber was made on April 30, 1896:

We are convinced that the Chamber embodies a Republican majority which is firmly resolved to set aside those questions that divide it in order to devote its attention to those democratic reforms which have been needed for some time and which we are now in a position to realize . . .

The best way to destroy revolutionary doctrines is to remain faithful to the ideals of justice and solidarity which are part of the Republican tradition.[33]

The Premier went on to discuss the problems of fiscal reform and a balanced budget and ended up with an appeal for appeasement:

> France is anxious to get down to work. She is tired of agitations and thirsts for peace and tranquility. She asks us to think of her and to rid ourselves of the dissensions which weaken us. We have assumed a heavy burden in order to serve the country. We are certain that you will understand this and respond to our appeal . . . in order to bring about a policy of peace and progress in the higher interests of the Republic.

Those who supported the ministry were afraid of being considered reactionaries, and Deschanel attempted to assuage this fear in a speech delivered at Marseilles on October 26, 1896:

> Is it true, as is asked every day, that those Republicans who are not Radicals or Socialists are interested only in maintaining the *status quo*? Is it true that only the Radicals and the Socialists are progressive and that France has only the choice between them and the reactionaries?
>
> I propose to show that this is not true. I propose to show that after all the reforms that we Opportunists have achieved in the past, we intend to achieve more. When we refused to follow the Radicals and the Socialists, it is not, as I often hear, because they are "going too fast too quickly" (one can never progress too quickly) but because they are going against history, science, and civilization. How often in the past in other countries have those who thought themselves "the wave of the future" been in reality an echo of the past. There are reactionaries of the Left just as there are reactionaries of the Right. We do not propose to be included among either.[34]

The assurance of Méline and his supporters that theirs was the true way was strengthened in 1896 by Opportunist successes in the municipal elections and by the visit of Tsar Nicholas II and

---

[33] Quoted in Daniel, *L'Année Politique,* 1896, p. 163.
[34] Deschanel, *La République nouvelle,* pp. 165–166.

the Tsarina to France in October of that year. The municipal elections showed that there were Opportunist majorities in the councils of 1,508 communes as opposed to Socialist majorities in 12 communes, Radical majorities in 373 communes, *Rallié* majorities in 91 communes, and Intransigent majorities in 328.[35] These figures seemed to indicate that there had been no change in voter sentiment since 1893. The visit of the Russian royal family crowned the efforts of France, which dated back to 1891, to achieve an alliance with Russia, thus ending the threat of a single-handed war with Germany. The fact that the visit was enthusiastically received by the great majority of Frenchmen could not help but add to the ministry's sense of accomplishment.

From April 1896 until the eve of the elections of 1898 the Opportunist leaders, with the exception of Isambert, were in agreement on the need for a disciplined majority and a stable government.[36] In speeches all over the country, Méline, Barthou, Poincaré, and Deschanel sounded this theme above all others, and in this period both Radicals and Opportunists began to organize political groups to strengthen party discipline. In 1895 Spuller founded the *Association Gambettiste,* in 1897 Waldeck-Rousseau started the *Grand Cercle Républicain,* and at the end of that year Waldeck-Rousseau and Poincaré founded the *Comité national républicain du commerce et de l'industrie.* It was the aim of these associations to establish a common electoral program and a uniform attitude toward political problems among the various candidates sponsored by them. Recognizing that diverse local conditions created differences of opinion among deputies bearing the same label, the associations tried to coordinate departmental activity within a general ideological framework. As Waldeck-Rousseau put it, "The aim of an association is to spread propaganda, to establish a line of communication between a central committee and committees in the departments. Another purpose is to organ-

[35] Daniel, *L'Année Politique,* 1896, p. 197.
[36] See *La République Française,* May 24, 1897.

ize lectures." [37] In attempting to create some sort of political organization the Opportunists were faced with virtually the same problems as Étienne Lamy.

Another Opportunist concern was the re-evaluation of the roles of the executive and the legislature, a concern which had its roots in the Panama scandal. Poincaré and Deschanel, speaking at Nogent-le-Rotrou on March 14, 1897, insisted that a proper balance between the two was essential for the maintenance of order. Said Poincaré:

The present government which we wholeheartedly support has already done a great deal under the direction of M. Méline to re-establish the idea of authority . . . If we do not want to slip into administrative chaos which inevitably leads to revolution and dictatorships, we must ardently support the prerogatives of the government, which far from being incompatible with liberty are the only means of preserving it.

Deschanel added that he had little confidence that the present Chamber would achieve these reforms. "We can not expect much from this legislature. We must look to the country and hope that it will respond." [38]

If the chief concern of the Opportunist leaders during the Méline era was the formation of a responsible conservative Republican party, what was their attitude toward the *Ralliement*? This was best summed up by Méline himself in a speech delivered in Remiremont in the Vosges on October 11, 1897 and quoted in *La République Française* on the following day. Having insisted that his ministry was not pursuing a "clerical" policy and that it had no intention of tampering with the Concordat or the laic laws, the Premier said, "The only thing which we refuse to do is to make war on religion, because if France does oppose clericalism, she is at the same time tolerant. We respect religion . . . Instead of quarrels we want appeasement in church-state relations." In

[37] Quoted in *Revue Politique et Parlementaire*, 5:246 (November 1897).

[38] Poincaré's and Deschanel's speeches quoted in *La République Française*, March 15, 1897.

answer to a favorite accusation aimed at him from the Left, Méline denied that his government had struck a bargain with the Right. "The Right votes with us because it prefers our policy to that of the Radicals and Socialists, and because it is putting the interests of the country above dynastic interests. The Right is not voting with us, it is voting against a social revolution which it has every right to do. In so doing it maintains complete independence from us." On the question of the *Ralliés* in the Chamber, Méline had this to say:

I am fully aware that the Radicals call Monarchists all those who have not always been Republicans. They contemptuously reject those who are known as *Ralliés* as if after twenty-seven years of the Republic it is still out of the question to open our ranks to such loyal and sincere men as our colleague, the Comte d'Alsace,[39] whose votes since he was elected a deputy have been, without exception, as Republican as ours. I say without hesitation that such support does honor to the government . . .

For a long time "concentration" was a trap for the Opportunists and yet they supported it loyally . . . We must cease to be equivocal because equivocation has done much harm in the past by making it impossible to establish a true governmental majority.

Méline's attitude toward the *Ralliés* was similar to that of Spuller and Casimir-Perier. As long as the *Ralliés* supported the Opportunist program wholeheartedly they were acceptable. The Remiremont speech was unique, however, in that a Republican Premier had publicly honored a *Rallié* deputy. This indicated how confident Méline was of his majority, for he showed no fear of retribution from the Radicals.

The fact that Méline considered the religious controversy to be a dead issue and that he was not afraid of the taunts of the Left was revealed in his attitude toward the Brest election in 1897. It will be remembered that the Abbé Gayraud, a Christian Democrat, had defeated the Comte de Blois in a by-election at Brest in

[39] The Comte d'Alsace was a *Rallié* deputy elected in a by-election in the Vosges in 1894.

January. Suspicion of clerical interference in this priest-ridden constituency had led the Chamber to form a commission headed by Gustave Isambert to investigate the election.[40] On July 6, 1897, the commission reported that there had been illegal clerical interference, and the Chamber was asked to invalidate the election. Three hundred and thirty-four deputies voted for invalidation, seventy opposed it, and ten abstained. Among those abstaining were seven *Ralliés* and three Opportunists—Ribot, Barthou, the Minister of the Interior, and Méline.[41] The abstention of a Republican minister on such an issue would have been unthinkable even a year earlier.

The Premier was as good as his word in not undertaking any alteration of the laic laws, and wherever the rights of the state seemed to be threatened, Méline leapt to their defense. Throughout the period of his ministry the Catholic newspapers complained that more priests' salaries were suspended than under any other ministry. Catholics were continually complaining that the ministry was making no concessions in return for the support that it was getting from the Right. In a letter written on December 26, 1896, to the Vice-President of the Chamber of Commerce in Toulouse, Constantin Manuel, Lamy complained, ". . . the Opportunists have conceded nothing. If they persist in this indifference to our grievances and rights there is no reason to concede more than they." [42]

The government was not inclined to pay much attention to the *Fédération électorale's* appeal for equal rights for the Church. Méline and other ministers assumed that Conservatives and Catholics alike were so horrified by the specter of socialism that they were willing to support the ministry without demanding any legislative changes. Warned *La Politique Nouvelle* of March 8, 1897: "Do not be fooled by the Opportunists who evoke the Socialist menace without saying anything about the laic laws."

[40] J. O., Chambre, *Débats* (March 4, 1897), p. 765.
[41] *Ibid.* (July 6, 1897), p. 845.
[42] Lamy papers.

Despite Méline's refusal to compromise on the question of the laws, he was under constant attack from the Left, particularly from the Radicals, who were themselves under considerable pressure to take a firm position on economic and social questions. Some, known as the Radical-Socialists and led by Goblet, wanted an alliance with the Socialists. Others, including Léon Bourgeois and Brisson, believed passionately in the principle of private property and were extremely suspicious of the views of Jaurès and Guesde. The Radicals, now very definitely in opposition, found it impossible to agree on economic and social questions. Only one issue united them and that was anticlericalism. Méline's policy of conciliation toward the Catholics was a godsend, and they did not hesitate to exploit it.[43]

The Radicals charged that the government was the prisoner of the Church and that republican institutions were in serious danger. Such accusations were embarrassing to the Opportunists, who never liked to have their Republican orthodoxy questioned. Although many, including Méline, were no longer bothered by these taunts, others in the government majority began to question Méline's policy of conciliation. These Opportunists joined the Radicals and Socialists in the vote to invalidate the election of the Abbé Gayraud. An anonymous writer in the *Revue Politique et Parlementaire,* which was sympathetic to Méline, complained that there was an increasing desire on the part of many Opportunists to return to the safe ground of "concentration."[44]

Rumors began to circulate early in 1898 that Louis Barthou, the Minister of the Interior, had fallen out with Méline on the question of a clear-cut break with the Radicals. The *Journal des Débats* of April 26, 1898, reported that Barthou had instructed

[43] Kayser, *Les Grandes batailles,* pp. 247–252.
[44] Anonymous, "Le Parti progressiste," *Revue Politique et Parlementaire,* 12:489 (June 1897).

the prefects to seek a pact with any Radicals who were not willing to form an alliance with the Socialists. Barthou denied this in his campaign speech at Oléron (Basses-Pyrénées) on April 24, 1898, but a comparison of campaign speeches of Opportunist leaders in the spring of 1898 reveals that there were crucial differences which divided the government majority and even the ministry. At Oléron, Barthou stressed the rights of the state:

We have not confused appeasement with abdication, or moderation with weakness. If we have, in the name of freedom of conscience, shown a healthy respect for the right of anyone to worship as he chooses, we have never ceased to be on guard against clericalism which uses religion as a means to destroy the rights of the state and which is an eternal enemy of the Republic. We have used the provisions of the Concordat to suppress any attempt to violate the civil state. What do they [the Radicals] want of us? What could they have done?

The country knows that the laic laws to which she is attached, which I have always proclaimed to be the honor and strength of the Republic and which I recently stated were an integral and inalienable part of the Republican domain, have always been respected by the ministry. We have no intention of barring the door to anyone. In fact we have welcomed those who have accepted the regime wholeheartedly. We want to warn the voters, however, against the perfidious designs of those who would enter the Republic to destroy it.[45]

This declaration of the inviolability of the laic laws could hardly be considered encouraging to the liberal Catholic elements which asked only that this principle not be mentioned. Barthou seemed more anxious to convince the Radicals rather than Lamy of the good intentions of the government.

Paul Deschanel's speech at Lyons on May 1, 1898, was no more encouraging from the point of view of the Catholics. He admitted that there was a change in the political structure of the country

---

[45] Quoted in Daniel, *L'Année Politique,* 1898, pp. 503–504.

and that what the voter had to choose between was the Republic
of Lamartine and Gambetta, on the one hand, and the Republic of
Louis Blanc and Clemenceau on the other. Then the future President of the Republic came to the question of the *Ralliés:*

Different political elements fall under the heading of *"Rallié."* We
must distinguish between the *Ralliés* in Parliament, who are either
the tools of the Church or who have reluctantly accepted the form of
government, and the large number of voters who have been coming
to the Republic since its establishment under the careful guidance
of Thiers, Gambetta and Carnot, to mention only the dead. We must
not confuse the *Ralliés* of the Chamber and the *Ralliés* in the country, very different one from the other, with the thousands of young
voters who are just becoming aware of public affairs, and who are
not *Ralliés* because they have never known any other regime or other
laws.

The essential fact is that although there are some who refuse to
recognize it, more and more sons of those who twenty years ago
voted for Monarchist candidates are voting for Republican candidates. This tendency is increasing and it is responsible for changing
the political structure of the country.[46]

Deschanel paid no attention to the statement of the Premier
which enthusiastically endorsed the adherence to the Republic
of men like the Comte d'Alsace. Although he made a distinction
between his politics and the politics of the Radicals, he refused
to identify himself with the Independent Republicans or with
the liberal element of the *Fédération électorale*. Deschanel's
speech at Lyons was typical of the reaction of an increasing number of Opportunists to the accusations of unorthodoxy which
came from the Left.

Méline's speech at Remiremont on April 18 reflected the feelings of those Opportunists who had once and for all rejected
"concentration." Again he spoke of the Socialist menace and
castigated the Radicals for flirting with it. "The greatest service
which I believe that I have done for the Republic," said the

[46] *La République Française,* May 2, 1898.

Premier, "is to have prevented its being consumed by revolution . . . thereby removing the last obstacle which stood in the way of many excellent Frenchmen who wished to rally to the Republic." [47] Government stability, he continued, made the Republic unquestionably more attractive:

It was because of this that there occurred this vast adherence to the Republic by those who once opposed it, an event which had been predicted and expected by Gambetta and Jules Ferry. I consider the *Ralliement* to be a great victory for the Republic, and I do not hesitate to declare that I am proud of it.

Méline refused to admit that his ministry was practicing a policy which favored clericalism:

We have always been respectful and conciliatory toward religion, and we have resisted the factious spirit which incites quarrels and which wants to weaken the whole idea of religion. We believe that this sort of thing weakens and disrupts the country. We have always chosen appeasement over intolerance.

On the other hand, when we have discovered violations of the Concordat such as political interference on the part of the clergy we have come quickly to the defense of the state.

Whereas Barthou and Deschanel stressed a militant defense of the Concordat and the laic laws, Méline emphasized appeasement. Barthou had talked of the inviolability of these laws. The Premier steered clear of a similar declaration. This was a clear indication that he had reached at least a tacit agreement with Étienne Lamy who, in agreement with the Vatican, had expressed the hope that Opportunist candidates would say nothing of the inviolability of the laic laws.

The basic difference between the two positions was that in the first, represented by Barthou, there was the fear that the ministry had gone too far with its conciliatory policy, thereby alienating the Radicals unnecessarily, while in the second, represented by Méline, there was the assumption that there was no further

[47] *Ibid.*, April 19, 1898.

quarrel with the Right, which either implicitly or explicitly supported the ministry. Méline's whole attention was focused on the
threat from the Left. But the more hostile he became toward
the Radicals and those who favored the revival of "concentration," the more essential it became for him to maintain the support of the Right. This was very different from the attitude of
the Opportunists on the eve of the elections of 1893.

It is difficult to ascertain with any precision whether Méline,
in his efforts to woo the Right, went beyond the mere refusal to
mention the unalterable nature of the laic laws. Until April 1898
he had been unwilling to consider any adjustments of the laws.
Yet there are indications that some in the ministry were willing
to go further in offering concessions. Leo XIII is quoted as saying that the historian Gabriel Hanotaux, Méline's foreign minister, had admitted that the government would support *Rallié*
candidates in the elections and might go even further if it did
not meet too much opposition from the Left.[48] Jacques Piou
claimed that Hanotaux was willing to permit optional religious
training in the primary schools after class and to permit seminary
students to serve in the medical corps in peace-time.[49] Whether
there was opposition to this scheme in the Cabinet or whether
Méline felt that such a concession would be too dangerous is not
known. The fact is that it was never mentioned to Lamy during
his meeting with Méline on April 3, 1898.

The ministry did decide, however, to support *Fédération* candidates in certain cases. Lamy wrote on March 16, "The Opportunists are becoming frightened, a bit late to be sure, by the
chaotic situation which they have created. They are now pro-
posing that we come to an agreement with them on a certain
number of points."[50] The administration did agree to support
Jacques Piou, which was quite a concession considering the

[48] See letter from the Abbé Bailly to the Abbé Picard, April 24, 1897, quoted in
Jarry, "L'Orientation politique de *La Croix*," p. 1050.
[49] Piou, *Albert de Mun*, pp. 173–174.
[50] Lamy to the Abbé Rembrand, March 16, 1898, Lamy papers.

attitude of the Opportunists toward the former leader of the *Ralliement* in 1893. A letter from Albert de Mun to Lamy on April 11, 1898, provides another example of cooperation between the government and the *Fédération*.

Before leaving for Finistère I would like to say something to you about a situation which interests me particularly, and with which you are, no doubt, *au courant*. It concerns our friend Flournoy [the *Fédération* candidate in Finistère] in Lorient who is opposed by M. Quyesse. I am told that the administration, or at least the sub-prefect, is giving its open support to the Republican candidate. This is typical of the discrepancy between the parliamentary politics of the last two years and the electoral politics of today. I am afraid that we will see many examples of it.[51]

De Mun wanted to know if Lamy could do something about Flournoy. Lamy was able to get a guarantee that the administration would remain absolutely neutral, which, in Brittany, was tantamount to support.[52]

De Mun's letter also reveals some of the problems which confronted the ministry in the spring of 1898. Not only was the support given to it by many Opportunist leaders beginning to waver, but it was also having difficulty with the prefects and subprefects who, after long years of religious quarrels, were trained to resist anything which smelled of clericalism. Méline found himself in a similar position to that of Étienne Lamy in that he was unable to establish control over local politics. As they entered the electoral fray in the spring of 1898, the Opportunists were far from being the disciplined and cohesive group they had thought themselves to be when they had emerged triumphant from the elections of 1893. In some departments, such as the Nord and the Pas-de-Calais, they allied with the *Ralliés;* in others, such as the Eure and the Cher, they fought them.[53]

---

[51] Lamy papers.
[52] De Mun to Lamy, April 14, 1898, Lamy papers.
[53] See *Le Figaro,* May 2, 1898.

The elections held on May 8 and 22 revealed that the Opportunists had gained four seats,[54] but Henri Avenel pointed out that one Opportunist candidate out of three favored "concentration." [55] On June 14 the new Chamber was presented with the following *ordre du jour:* "The Chamber approves the declaration of the Government and will support a policy of democratic reform sponsored by a union of all Republicans." [56] This *ordre du jour* was accepted by five hundred and twenty-seven deputies and opposed by only two. Even the Intransigents, anxious to save Méline, voted for it. Then Léon Bourgeois and Henri Ricard tacked on an amendment to the *ordre du jour* to the effect that the ministry would have to be supported by an exclusively Republican majority.[57] This was carried by two hundred and ninety-five votes to two hundred and forty-six, and Méline submitted his resignation that evening.

The fall of Méline was a victory for the forces in favor of "concentration" within the Opportunist majority. The succeeding ministries revived the pattern which was more agreeable to the many Republican deputies who did not like striking out in new directions. Méline had ventured too far in his endorsement of the *Ralliement.* Many Opportunists considered him to be a tool of the Right. Poincaré, who did not break with him until the spring of 1899 during the climax of the Dreyfus Affair, had this to say about the man whose political views he had until recently endorsed:

I can not admit that a party can exist without common ideals, without a program or which accepts as a program the resistance to socialism.
You have around you—in spite of you, no doubt—people with whom I could never associate . . . Instead of letting you be the head

[54] Daniel, *L'Année Politique,* 1898, p. 217.
[55] Avenel, *Le Nouveau ministère et la nouvelle chambre,* p. 254.
[56] Quoted in Daniel, *L'Année Politique,* 1898, p. 241.
[57] *Ibid.,* p. 242.

of a party, they want to make you a prisoner of a reactionary coalition . . . Those who have fought at your side deplore this.[58]

Méline was ostracized by the ruling circles of the Republic from 1898 until the World War. The fate of the former associate of Gambetta was similar to that of the Left-Centrists in 1885. He and other old Opportunists were guilty of having harbored unorthodox views on anticlericalism.

[58] Poincaré to Méline, May 20, 1899 quoted in Fernand Payen, *Poincaré chez lui* (Paris, 1936), pp. 427–428.

CONCLUSION

 There can be no doubt that the *Ralliement* succeeded in bringing many French citizens who had supported anti-Republican candidates in the past to accept the Republic. Republican gains in normally Conservative and Catholic areas testify to this fact. A new generation was coming of age in the 1890's which considered the constitutional squabbles of the early years of the Third Republic to be unimportant. The *Ralliement* also succeeded in destroying the *Union des droites,* although the inability of the Conservatives to unite effectively and lack of interest on the part of the electorate in obsolete conflicts contributed to its demise. The movement failed, however, to achieve its two major purposes: to associate the French government with Vatican efforts to solve the Roman Question and, more important, to help bring about a realignment of forces in the political structure of France.

If Leo XIII hoped to achieve some sort of rapprochement with France, he could not afford to antagonize the Opportunists; hence he could not insist on immediate revision of the laic laws. He adopted a policy of conciliation designed to remove Republican prejudices against the Church which, unfortunately, created a misunderstanding between the Vatican and major Catholic elements in France. The clergy, influential laymen, and the Catholic press were not agreeable to the idea of postponing their futile campaign to revise the laws.

It has been suggested that the timing of the toast in Algiers in 1890 and the papal encyclical of 1892 was poor in that the French Catholics were not as yet prepared to accept a policy of appeasement.[1] It is difficult, however, to accept this view if the political situation in France at that time is taken into account. The Right was discredited and desperately in need of a way out of its difficulties. The Opportunists, anxious to consolidate the gains of the 1880's and to maintain their dominant political position, were willing to be conciliatory toward the Right. The Church was open to new onslaughts of anticlericalism because some members of the clergy had been involved in the Boulangist campaign. Socialism was beginning to make headway among the working classes, causing grave concern in conservative circles. The economic and social problems confronting the Western world at the end of the nineteenth century demanded new political attitudes. Finally, France was isolated and badly in need of an ally to counterbalance the Triple Alliance. The Vatican had the opportunity of playing an important role in bringing about essential changes in the country and in so doing to help its own cause. There can be no doubt that the toast and encyclical were timed to coincide with the political ferment in France.

It is within the French body politic that one must seek the causes for the failure of the *Ralliement*. The threat from the Left, increased by the possibility of a union between Radicals and Socialists, made it all the more essential for conservatives to come to some kind of understanding. Even the Intransigents felt that they could cooperate with Republicans on a day-to-day basis without compromising their inner convictions. For this reason they supported Méline, whom they considered to be a bulwark against Socialism. The *Ralliés* were willing to renounce their convictions in order to facilitate the formation of a "Tory" party within the framework of the Republic. Most Opportunists realized that "concentration" was outmoded and that it was necessary

---

[1] Canon Roger Aubert, Professor of Church History at the University of Louvain, who is currently writing a history of Leo XIII's pontificate for the Fliche-Martin series, feels that the timing of the *Ralliement* was poor in that the French clergy was not prepared for it. He explained this to me in a conversation which I had with him at Louvain in May 1961.

to create a stronger government supported by a homogeneous majority capable of preserving the *status quo*. But, as is often the case in France, the feeling for tradition was stronger than the feeling for innovation. It seemed simpler for all concerned to cling to the old, established ways rather than to adopt new ones.

The Intransigents could not take the final step of entering the Republic. Even when the *Droite constitutionnelle* threatened to destroy the *Union des droites* by splitting it in half, the Intransigents were unwilling to save the one organization which had given the Right some semblance of unity. They preferred to sacrifice their political life in order to do honor to an exiled pretender whose chances of a restoration had long since become impossible.

Jacques Piou and his followers hesitated too long in identifying themselves with the Republic. It can be said in their behalf that they preferred to act slowly in order to bring with them as many Conservatives as possible. A mass entrance of Conservatives into the Republic would have been extremely effective. Piou's hesitation, however, did nothing to convince the Intransigents and only irritated the Opportunists by creating the impression that the members of the *Droite constitutionnelle* were reluctant to relinquish their former political attitudes.

The destruction of the *Union des droites* forced French Catholics to fend for themselves. Although the *Ralliement* stimulated considerable enthusiasm for political action among them, as evidenced by their activity between 1893 and 1898, it could not unify them as Leo XIII had so fervently hoped. Centuries of strife among Gallicans and Ultramontanes, Jansenists and Jesuits, Liberals and Conservatives could not be easily forgotten. The *Ralliement* served only to underline deep-seated disagreements. Conservative Catholics could not comprehend the need to come to terms with the modern world. Political action was for them an unceasing effort to restore the Church to its former position of prestige. Liberal Catholics, on the other hand, recognized the fact that the Church could survive in France only if Catholics and Republicans tolerated each other. Because of the profound disagreements among French Catholics the *Fédération électorale* suffered the same fate as the *Union des droites*.

The critical issue in terms of the *Ralliement* was whether the laic laws should be accepted by Catholics and Conservatives. Intransigents in both groups fervently believed that they had to fight at all cost for the abrogation of these laws. Piou and Lamy were soon aware that if the *Ralliement* were to succeed, Catholics and Conservatives would have to have the cooperation of the Opportunists, and in this they were in agreement with the Vatican. Such cooperation could be obtained only if the laic laws were accepted, at least temporarily. Piou came to this conclusion reluctantly, early in 1893. Most of the members of the *Droite constitutionnelle,* which in that year became the *Droite républicaine,* said nothing about the laws in their campaign speeches either in 1893 or in 1898. Although Lamy also realized that in most cases it would be impossible to demand more of Opportunist candidates than the omission of any statement referring to the intangibility of the laws, he was willing to allow Catholics to ask for more in areas where they thought that they could get it. Piou, in his history of the *Ralliement,* blamed Lamy for the failure of the movement because he felt that the *Fédération électorale* had insisted on revision of the laic laws.[2] Like so many others, Piou associated the *Fédération* with the activities of the Assumptionists and the Rheims group. But Lamy, in a letter written to Piou on June 27, 1898, just after the fall of the Méline ministry, insisted that he had never asked for more than he thought he could get. "Both you and I" he wrote, "have struggled vigorously wherever we could without compromising those interests which we are committed to defend. Neither of us has ever pursued a policy which could not get results."[3]

[2] Piou, *Le Ralliement,* pp. 74–75.
[3] Lamy papers.

Catholic and Conservative *Ralliés* who followed Lamy and Piou in adopting a policy of appeasement were in effect accepting the fact that a realignment of political forces was necessary. In order for the Ralliement to succeed they had to persuade the nation of the importance of the movement. To do this the *Ralliés* needed young, vigorous, and effective leadership. This they lacked. Piou had been too involved in the machinations of the Right during the Boulanger crisis, he hesitated too long before adhering to the Republic, and he had failed to be re-elected in 1893. Lamy was never able to dominate the *Fédération électorale* or attract much attention to his cause. He had refused to attend the Catholic congresses of 1896 and 1897 because he did not want to be too closely identified with "Catholic" political activity. This resulted in his remaining relatively unknown with the *Fédération*. Henri Joly, a political commentator sympathetic to the *Ralliement,* put his finger on a fatal flaw in the movement:

> The policy of appeasement had the misfortune of being new. I thought once that this would give it an advantage, but I was cruelly disappointed. Novelty and youth are attractive when they appeal to the young at heart who are impatient to act and to cooperate with those who are willing to help them achieve their ends. Novelty has no value when it is advocated by the unimaginative and the disillusioned. Then it becomes suspect.[4]

The Opportunists were as incapable of coming to grips with a new political situation as were the Catholics and Conservatives. Most of them realized the need for a homogeneous majority which would ultimately lead to stronger government. But when it came to incorporating Conservatives who were willing to adhere to the Republic into this majority, it was more than some Opportunists could take, for it opened them to the charge of not being orthodox Republicans. And Radicals who found it hard to stomach an alliance with the Socialists found that they

---

[4] Henri Joly, *Histoire électorale de 1893* (Paris, 1894), p. 26.

could make common cause with these Opportunists. As the possibility of creating a two-party system within the Republic became increasingly obvious, the more nostalgic Republicans of both groups became for the good old days of "concentration." Thus in the end the traditional political habit won out.

A major problem for Lamy, Méline, and Piou in their struggle to overcome tradition was the obstinacy of local politicians. Between 1896 and 1898, when Lamy was in the process of organizing the *Fédération électorale* into a centralized group, he ran counter to local sentiment, which distrusted any sort of centralization. Méline found that it was very difficult to impose his policy on the local level where prefect and subprefect were incapable of understanding the idea of being tolerant toward the Catholics. Piou, in attempting to establish the *Droite constitutionnelle* on the local level, found himself constantly in conflict with established Conservative organizations. It was impossible to introduce new political attitudes into the provinces, where traditions were solidly entrenched.

The Dreyfus Affair can in no way be considered a cause for the failure of the *Ralliement,* but there is a very definite connection between the two movements. Dreyfus was arrested in 1894 during the brief period when Casimir-Perier was President of the Republic. The campaign for revision began in the months before the elections of 1898. Events important to both movements were interwoven. The Dreyfus Affair is linked to the *Ralliement* in that the attitude of the various political elements in France toward the Affair were shaped to a large extent by their reaction to the *Ralliement.*

To the Intransigents the attacks on the glorious French army were further examples of the Republic's lack of responsibility. The Assumptionists immediately assumed that Dreyfus and the "Jewish syndicate" were bent upon destroying the Church. The Affair provided them with the occasion to sound a call to arms, an occasion they had been waiting for since the encyclical *Au milieu des sollicitudes.*[5] In general all the anti-Republican elements which had opposed the *Ralliement* considered themselves vindicated by the Affair.

Those who were badly hurt by the Affair were the supporters of the *Ralliement.*[6] They looked upon the revisionist campaign as an attempt to destroy the *"esprit nouveau." Le Petit Moniteur,* which supported Méline, commented on Zola's trial on February 20, 1898 as follows:

At the time when appeasement was beginning to make itself felt in the country after a long period of factious quarrels, a small group of malcontents has taken advantage of an incident to excite and trouble people on behalf of the Dreyfus syndicate. This syndicate has gathered in all those who are not satisfied.

The Affair itself has become less important. The Méline Ministry has become the focal point for passionate attacks from those who support the syndicate. Those who oppose the return of intolerant and sectarian politicians are also the object of attack from the syndicate.

The *Journal des Débats,* which voiced the sentiments of the Left-Centrists and which supported Méline and the *"esprit nouveau,"* had this to say on February 25, 1898, about Zola's sentence:

Yesterday's verdict has given us hope that there will be an end to the recent troubles. Justice has been done. Passions must subside, and a spirit of appeasement must prevail. We also hope that all those in positions of authority and responsibility will make every effort to safeguard order, peace and justice.

La République Française, the staunch supporter of Méline, who had been its editor-in-chief until he took office in 1896, had this to say on February 9, 1898, about the campaign for revision:

[5] Pierre Micquel, *L'Affaire Dreyfus* (Paris, 1959), p. 53. This little volume, published in the *Que sais-je* series, is among the more balanced and objective analyses of the case.

[6] *Ibid.,* p. 121.

The Dreyfus Affair . . . provides an opportunity for the Radicals and Socialists to interpellate the government *ad infinitum* and to initiate continuous debates in the Chamber. When they accept as a principle of government the confusion of powers, when they involve in politics questions related to the judiciary, when they attempt to drag the ministers who are part of the executive branch into the controversy, they at least have the obligation to tell the electorate what they would do if they succeeded in overthrowing the ministry.

. . . Have we not always said that throughout this affair the Left has been trying to induce a ministerial crisis?

At Remiremont Méline developed this theme on the eve of the elections of 1898:

Our majority has recently permitted us to overcome a crisis which threatened the security of the country. We overcame this crisis because we were sincere and because we respected the law and legal processes of this nation. We are also attached to that great institution, the army, which symbolizes our most cherished hopes and which provides the bonds which unite all Frenchmen.[7]

For Méline and his supporters the Affair was an effort on the part of the Left to confuse the situation and to prevent the realignment of the French political structure.

Finally the Affair provided those who wished to revive "concentration" with an excellent opportunity for pronouncing the Republic in danger. They called for the union of all orthodox Republicans to defend it. Once again the familiar battle cry of 1885 and 1889 was sounded. The inevitable result of "concentration," which was revived after the fall of the Méline ministry, was further attacks on the Church.

The *Ralliement* was more than anything else an attempt on the part of the French body politic to readjust to new conditions. The Dreyfus Affair served to strengthen the position of the traditionalists within all the political groups by providing them with the excuse to revive old attitudes and habits.

[7] *La République Française,* April 19, 1898.

Appendixes

Bibliography

Index

APPENDIX A

The list of deputies who were original members of the *Droite constitutionnelle* founded in 1890.

D'Arenberg (Cher)
Brincard (Seine-et-Oise)
Delafosse (Calvados)
Desjardins (Aisne)
Desjardins-Verkinder (Nord)
De l'Aigle (Oise)
Frescheville (Nord)
Hély d'Oissel (Seine-et-Oise)

De Montéty (Aveyron)
De Montsaulnin (Cher)
Morillot (Marne)
Le Gavrien (Nord)
Paulmier (Calvados)
Piou (Haute-Garonne)
Renard (Nord)
Thellier de Poncheville (Nord)

APPENDIX B

Rallié deputies elected in 1893, their occupation and interests.

Aisne
Desjardins (Industrialist)
Firino (First election—Landowner)

Basses-Alpes
D'Hugues (First election—Landowner—anti-Semite)

Ardèches
De Vogüé (First election—Landowner—Literary critic and member
   of the *Académie Française*—Interested in reform of the laic laws)

Ardennes
De Wignancourt

Calvados
Delafosse (Landowner—Interested in reform of the laic laws)
Paulmier (Landowner)

Charente-Inf.
Dufaure (First election—Landowner—Interested in reform of the
   laic laws)

Corsica
Antoine Gavini
Sébastien Gavini (First election)

Cher
D'Arenberg (Landowner—Chairman of the board of the Suez Company—Primarily interested in colonial matters)

Eure
Passy (Primarily interested in financial matters)

Indre
Balsan (Industrialist)

Loire-Atlantique
Amaury-Simon (First election)

Maine-et-Loire
De Grandmaison (First election—Landowner)

Haute-Marne
Bourlon de Rouvre (Interested in agricultural questions)

Nièvre
Jaluzot (Industrialist)

Nord
Le Gavrien (Landowner and industrialist)
Des Rotours (Industrialist)
De Montalembert (Nephew of the great Liberal Catholic, Charles
    de Montalembert (1800–1870)—Landowner—Interested in reform
    of the laic laws)
Loyer (First election)
Plichon (Champion of protectionism)
Lemire (Christian Democrat—First election—Interested in reform of
    the laic laws)

Orne
De Mackau (Leader of the *Union des droites* whose adherence to the
    Republic in 1892 was detrimental to the Right—Advocate of greater
    local autonomy and the right for priests to teach in Primary Schools
    in Catholic communities)

Pas de Calais
Adam (Interested in agricultural questions)
Dussaussoy (First election—Landowner)
Tailliandier (Landowner—Interested in reform of the laic laws)

Hautes-Pyrénées
Achille Fould (Member of distinguished banking family whose father
    was a Minister of Finance under Napoleon III)

Belfort
Vieillard (First election—Demanded reform of the laic laws)

Saône-et-Loire
Schneider (Member of great industrial family)

Sarthe
Galpin (Landowner)

Seine (9th arrondissement)
Berry (First election)

Seine-Inf.
De Montfort (Landowner—Primarily interested in military matters)

Seine-et-Oise
Brincard (Industrialist)

Tarne
Reille (Mining interests)

Vienne
Dupuytrem (Landowner)

BIBLIOGRAPHY

I. UNPUBLISHED PRIMARY SOURCES

The Lamy Papers

These consist of the notebooks and correspondence of Étienne Lamy who was the political leader of the *Ralliement* between 1896–1898. The papers are in the possession of M. Dominique Audollent of Clermont-Ferrand, and they cover most of the phases of Lamy's life: his career as a deputy (1871–1881), his struggle against anticlericalism in the 1880's, the *Ralliement,* as well as papers relating to the *Académie Française* of which he was a member from 1905 to 1919. Although available to the interested scholar, these papers have not been examined extensively by anyone other than myself.

Of particular interest to anyone studying the *Ralliement* are a notebook in which Lamy copied letters to Cardinals Perraud, Langénieux, and Rampolla, and from Rampolla, Perraud, and Langénieux to Lamy; letters from Mgr. Mourey, Auditor of the Rota, which reflect the feelings and attitudes of key figures in the Vatican during the period of the *Ralliement;* and finally, correspondence from Catholics in the provinces during the period when Lamy was head of the *Fédération électorale,* which reflect the feelings in the provinces toward the movement.

Archives Nationales

The archives of the now defunct *Ministère des Cultes* (F 19 series) are of particular interest to the students of Church-State relations in France throughout the nineteenth century. The following cartons pertain to the *Ralliement:*

F 19 1943 Franco-Vatican relations, 1881–1891.

F 19 1944 Franco-Vatican relations, 1891–1905.

F 19 5610 The attitude of the French clergy toward the Third Republic.

F 19 5612–5613 Reaction of the French clergy to the Toast of Cardinal Lavigerie at Algiers in 1890.

F 19 5616 Papers pertaining to the Gouthe-Soulard crisis.
F 19 5565 The attitude of the Catholic press toward the Republic, 1895–1898.
F 19 5620 The attitude of the French clergy toward the elections of 1898.

2. PUBLISHED PRIMARY SOURCES

Journal Officiel, Débats, Chambre, 1890–1898.
Rapport fait au nom de la Commission chargée de réunir et de publier les textes authentiques des programmes et engagements électoraux des députés. VIe Législature (Paris, 1894).

Newspapers

La Croix, 1890–1898.
La Croix du Gers, 1898.
La Croix du Nord, 1893, 1898.
Le Dépêche du Nord, 1893, 1898.
La Droite Républicaine, 1886–1887.
L'Éclair, 1890–1893.
Le Figaro, 1889–1899.
La France Nouvelle, 1891–1893.
Journal des Débats, 1890–1898.
La Liberté des Hautes-Pyrénées, 1892–1898.
L'Observateur Français, 1890–1893.
Le Petit Moniteur, 1896–1898.
Le Petit Moniteur Universel, 1890–1893.
La République Française, 1889–1899.
Le Temps, 1889–1899.
L'Union Nationale, 1894–1898.
L'Union Nationale de Bordeaux, 1894–1898.
L'Univers, 1890–1898.

Periodicals

L'Année Politique, 1889–1899.
Le Correspondant, 1890–1898.
La Nouvelle Revue, 1890–1898.
La Politique Nouvelle, 1896–1898.
La Quinzaine, 1894–1898.
La Revue des Deux Mondes, 1890–1898.

La Revue de Paris, 1896–1898.
La Revue Politique et Parlementaire, 1894–1898.

Books and pamphlets

Anonymous, *À Quoi sert la droite?* Paris, 1893.
———— *Du Toast à l'encyclique.* Paris: Lecoffre, 1892.
———— *Indifférence en matière politique et le parti catholique.* Paris, 1897.
———— *Les Intérêts catholiques en 1891.* Paris, 1891.
Avenel, Henri. *Annuaire de la presse française, 1895.* Paris: Librairies-imprimeries réunies, 1896.
———— *Comment vote la France. 18 ans de suffrage universel.* Paris: Librairies-imprimeries réunies, 1894.
———— *Le Nouveau ministère et la nouvelle chambre.* Paris: Flammarion, 1898.
Benoist, Charles. "La France et le Pape Léon XIII," *Revue des Deux Mondes,* 116:397–430 (March–April 1893).
———— *La Politique.* Paris: L. Chailley, 1894.
———— *La République nouvelle.* Paris: Alcan-Lévy, 1893.
Berthout, P. C. "Le clergé français et le peuple à la fin du xixe siècle," *Revue du Clergé français,* 18:25–46 (March 1899).
Bertrand, Alphonse. *La Chambre de 1889.* Paris: L. H. May 1890.
———— *La Chambre de 1893.* Paris: L. H. May 1894.
———— *La Chambre de 1898.* Paris: L. H. May 1899.
Blondel, Louis. *La Politique libérale et les libéraux.* Arras: Imprimerie moderne, 1896.
Boinvilliers, E. *Le Petit manuel du conservateur.* Paris: C. Schlaeber, 1891.
Bonjean, Jules. "Le Mouvement catholique et la politique générale," *Nouvelle Revue,* 72:673–690 (October 1891).
———— "La Dernière encyclique et la politique d'apaisement," *Nouvelle Revue,* 75:267–278 (March 1892).
Bosq, Paul, *Nos chers souverains.* Paris: F. Juven, 1898.
Bourloton, Edgar, Gaston Cougney, Adolphe Robert, eds. *Dictionnaire des parlementaires français, comprennant tous les membres des Assemblées françaises et tous les ministères français depuis le mai 1er 1789 jusqu'au 1er mai 1889,* 4 vols. Paris: Bourloton, 1891.
Broglie, Albert de. "L'Église et la France moderne," *Revue des Deux Mondes,* 141:283–319 (May 1897).

Bourgeois, Léon. "Vues politiques," *Revue de Paris,* 7:449–466 (April 1898).

Carnoy, Henry. *Dictionnaire des hommes du Nord.* Paris: Armorial français, 1899.

Castellane, Boniface de. "Une équivoque politique; les ralliés," *Nouvelle Revue,* 105:489–498 (April 1897).

Cochin, Denys. "Vues politiques," *Revue de Paris,* 7:511–523, April 1898).

Congrès National de la démocratie chrétienne tenu à Lyon du 25 au 30 novembre 1896, compte rendu. Lyons, 1896.

Compte-rendu général du congrès national catholique tenu à Rheims du 21 au 25 octobre 1896. Lille, 1897.

Congrès national catholique 1897. Compte rendu. Paris, 1897.

Coubertin, Pierre de. *L'Évolution française sous la Troisième République.* Paris: Plon, Nourrit, 1896.

Delafosse, Jules. *Discours et compte-rendus de Jules Delafosse 1890–1898,* 2 vols. Paris: P. Dupont, 1893–1898.

Deschanel, Paul. *Questions actuelles.* Paris: Hetzel, n.d.

———— *La République nouvelle.* Paris: C. Lévy, 1898.

Didon, P. *L'Union des catholiques de l'Église de France.* Paris: Plon, Nourrit, 1892.

Dietz, Jules. "Jules Ferry et les traditions républicaines," *Revue Politique et Parlementaire,* 161:121–141 (October 1934).

Fleury, Paul. *La Politique d'apaisement.* Paris, 1890.

Grenier, A. S. *Nos Deputés 1893–1898.* Paris: Berger-Lerrault, 1898.

Haget, A. *De la Constitution d'un nouveau parti.* Nevers: Mazeron, 1896.

Jay, Pierre. *La Politique pontificale et la presse française.* Lyons: "Salut Publique," 1893.

Joly, Henri. *Histoire électorale de 1893.* Paris: "La Réforme sociale," 1894.

Keller, Émile. *Les Élections de 1898.* Paris: Soye, 1897.

Laffitte, Jean-Paul. *Le Parti modéré.* Paris: A. Colin, 1896.

Lamy, Étienne, "La Politique religieuse du parti républicain," *Revue des Deux Mondes,* 58:293–328 (January 1887).

Lamy, Étienne. "Le Devoir des conservateurs," *Revue des Deux Mondes,* 3:512–536 (May–June 1892).

———— *Les Catholiques et la situation présente.* Paris, 1898.

Lapeyre, P. *Les Partis conservateurs et le clergé devant les leçons du scrutin.* Paris: Savaeté, 1899.

Lapparent, A. de. *Le Devoir de la concentration*. Paris: Soye, 1897.

Lecomte, Maxime. *Les Ralliés. Histoire d'un parti*. Paris: Flammarion, 1899.

Lecoq, C. *La République cléricale. Socialistes chrétiens et ralliés*. Paris: Léon, 1898.

Leroy-Beaulieu, A. "La République et les conservateurs," *Revue des Deux Mondes,* 98:84–122 (March–April 1890).

Leroy-Beaulieu, Paul. *Un Chapitre des moeurs électorales en France 1889–1890*. Paris: De Chaix, 1890.

Long, A. *Le Péril clérical*. Paris: Fischbacher, 1898.

Mackau, A. F. de. *L'Union, préface de la victoire*. Paris: Warmont, 1889.

Marcère, Edouard de. "l'Esprit nouveau," *Nouvelle Revue,* 88:5–21 (May 1894).

Méline, Jules. *Discours aux progressistes*. Paris: Association nationale républicaine, 1899.

Mermeix. *Les Coulisses du Boulangisme*. Paris: Cerf, 1890.

Muèl, Léon. *Tableau synoptique de tous les ministères de la Troisième République*. Paris: Pedone, 1908.

――― *Les Crises ministérielles de 1895 à 1898*. Paris: Mouillot, 1899.

Ollivier, Émile. *Solutions politiques et sociales*. Paris: Bellier, 1894.

Peccadut, J. *Les Catholiques. Une étude politique et sociale*. Paris: Dentu, 1896.

Perraud, Cardinal Adolphe-Louis. *Quelques réflexions au sujet de l'encyclique*. Paris: Poussièlgue, 1892.

Picot, Georges. "La Pacification religieuse 1832–92," *Revue des Deux Mondes,* 112:842–869 (July 1892).

――― "Les Bienfaits de la concentration," *Nouvelle Revue,* 1:161–168 (November 1899).

Poincaré, Raymond. "Vues politiques," *Revue de Paris,* 7:638–658 (April 1898).

Pressensé, Francis de. "La République et la crise du libéralisme," *Revue des Deux Mondes,* 139:765–804 (January 1897).

Reille, André. *Avant la bataille*. Notre-Dame de Montligeon: Imprimerie de Notre-Dame de Montligeon, 1897.

Reinach, Joseph. *La Politique opportuniste 1880–1889*. Paris: Charpentier, 1890.

Rémy de Simony, Henri. *Le Parti conservateur et son avenir*. Lille: Ducoulombier, 1885.

――― *La République ouverte*. Paris: Carré, 1891.

Ribeyre, Félix. *La Nouvelle chambre 1889–1893.* Paris: Dentu, 1890.

Roger, Jules. *Appel aux conservateurs.* Le Havre: Brindeau, 1891.

Salles, A. "Les Députés sortants 1893–1898," *Revue Politique et Parlementaire,* 16:33–79 (April–June 1898).

Simon, Georges. *Le Manuel de l'électeur.* Paris: Marchesson, 1898.

Spuller, Eugène. *L'Évolution politique et sociale de l'Église.* Paris: F. Alcan, 1893.

—— "La Politique de Léon XIII a-t-elle échouée?" *Revue de Paris,* 1:676–696 (February 1896).

—— "Quatorze mois de la législature," *Revue Politique et Parlementaire,* 3:1–21 (January 1895).

Thellier de Poncheville, Charles. *Les Catholiques en France.* Châlons-sur-Marne: Martin frères, 1892.

—— *Droits et devoirs des catholiques.* Châlons-sur-Marne: Martin frères, 1898.

Teste, Louis. *Les Monarchistes sous la Troisième République.* Paris: Rousseau, 1891.

Waldeck-Rousseau, René. *Opinions de M. Waldeck-Rousseau.* Paris, 1902.

3. SECONDARY SOURCES

Acomb, Evelyn M. *The French Laic Laws 1879–1889.* New York: Columbia University Press, 1941.

Anonymous. *Eugène Spuller 1835–1896.* Évreux, 1903.

Barbier, Émmanuel. *Histoire du catholicisme libéral et du catholicisme social,* 5 vols. Bordeaux: Cadoret, 1924.

Baunard, Louis. *Léon XIII et le toast d'Alger: Souveniris et documents de deux audiences pontificales intimes le 24 et le 26 Avril 1896.* Paris: J. de Gigord, 1914.

Beau de Loménie, Émmanuel. *Les Responsibilités des dynasties bourgeoises,* vol. II: *De MacMahon à Poincaré.* Paris: Denoël, 1947.

Boussel, Patrice. *L'Affaire Dreyfus et la presse.* Paris: A. Colin, 1960.

Byrnes, Robert F. "The French Christian Democrats in the 1890's; Their Appearance and their failure," *Catholic Historical Review,* 36:286–306 (October 1950).

—— *Anti-Semitism in Modern France.* New Brunswick: Rutgers University Press, 1950.

Cambon, Henri, ed. *Correspondance de Paul Cambon 1870–1924,* 2 vols. Paris: Grasset, 1940.

Capéran, Louis. *L'Anticléricalisme et l'affaire Dreyfus*. Toulouse: Imprimerie régionale, 1948.

Chapman, Guy. *The Dreyfus Case*. New York: Reynal, 1956.

—— *The Third Republic of France: the First Phase 1871–1894*. New York: St. Martin's Press, 1962.

Chastenet, Jacques. *Histoire de la Troisième République,* 7 vols. Paris: Hachette, 1952–1963.

Cheyssac, Léon de. *Le Ralliement*. Paris: Librairie des Sts.-Pères, 1906.

Cornilleau, Robert. *De Waldeck-Rousseau à Poincaré*. Paris: "Spes," 1926.

—— *Le Ralliement a-t-il échoué?* Paris: "Spes," 1927.

—— *L'Abbé Naudet*. Paris: "Spes," 1935.

Dabry, Pierre. *Les Catholiques républicains 1890–1903*. Paris: Chevalier et Rivière, 1905.

Dansette, Adrien. *Le Boulangisme 1886–1890*. Paris: Perrin, 1938.

—— *Les Affaires de Panama*. Paris: Perrin, 1934.

—— *Histoire religieuse de la France contemporaine,* 2 vols. Paris: Flammarion, 1951.

—— "Léon XIII et la politique du Ralliement," *Revue de Paris,* 58:103–114 (April 1951).

Debidour, A. *L'Église et l'état sous la Troisième République,* 2 vols. Paris: F. Alcan, 1906.

Denais, Joseph. *Un Apôtre de la liberté, Jacques Piou*. Paris: La Nef, 1959.

Dimier, Louis. *Vingt ans de l'Action Française*. Paris: Nouvelle librairie nationale, 1926.

Domenach, Jean-Marie. "Conscience politique et conscience religieuse," *L'Esprit,* 3:337–358 (March 1958).

Earle, Edward M., ed. *Modern France*. Princeton: Princeton University Press, 1951.

Ferrata, Dominique. *Ma Nonciature en France*. Paris: Action Populaire, 1922.

Fichaux, Louis. *Dom Sébastien Wyart*. Lille: Giard, 1910.

Freycinet, Charles de. *Souvenirs 1878–1898,* 2nd ed. Paris: Delagrave, 1913.

Goguel, François. *Géographie des élections françaises de 1870 à 1951*. Paris: A. Colin, 1951.

—— *La Politique des partis sous la Troisième République,* 3rd ed. Paris: Éditions du Seuil, 1957.

Gross, Robert D. *Liberal Catholicism in America.* Cambridge, Mass.: Harvard University Press, 1958.

Guillemin, Henri. *Histoire des catholiques françaises.* Geneva: Milieu du Monde, 1947.

Halévy, Daniel. *Pour l'Étude de la Troisième République.* Paris: Grasset, 1927.

Halasz, Nicolas. *Captain Dreyfus: The Story of a Mass Hysteria.* New York: Simon and Schuster, 1955.

Havard de la Montagne, Robert. *Le Ralliement.* Lille: Desclée, 1913.

―――― *Histoire de la démocratie chrétienne.* Paris: Amiot-Dumont, 1948.

Heuzey-Goyau, J.-Ph. *Georges Goyau.* Paris: 1947.

Jarry, Eugène. "L'Orientation politique de *La Croix* entre les années 1895–1900," *La Documentation Catholique,* 1154: 1031–1059 (August 23, 1954).

Kayser, Jacques. *Les Grandes batailles du radicalisme.* Paris: Rivière et Cie., 1962.

Lachapelle, Georges. *Le Ministère Méline.* Paris: A. Colin, 1928.

Lamy, Étienne. *Au Service des idées et des lettres.* Paris: Bloud, 1909.

―――― *Quelques oeuvres et quelques ouvriers.* Paris: Bloud, 1911.

Langer, William L. *The Franco-Russian Alliance, 1890–94.* Cambridge, Mass.: Harvard University Press, 1929.

Larkin, M. J. M. "The French Catholics and the Question of the Separation of Church and State," unpub. diss. Cambridge University, 1958.

Laudet, Fernand. *Soixante ans de souvenirs.* Paris: Bloud et Gay, 1934.

Le Bras, Gabriel. *Introduction à l'histoire de la pratique religieuse en France,* 2 vols. Paris: P. U. F., 1944–1948.

Lecanuet, E. *L'Église de France sous la Troisième République,* vol. II, *Pontificat de Léon XIII 1878–1894.* Paris: F. Alcan, 1910.

―――― *Les Signes avant-coureurs de la séparation.* Paris: F. Alcan, 1930.

―――― *La Vie de l'église sous Léon XIII.* Paris: F. Alcan, 1930.

Livre Blanc du Saint-Siège. La Séparation de l'Église et l'état en France. Paris: Poussièlgue, 1906.

Lynch, Miriam. *The Organized Social Apostolate of Albert de Mun.* Washington: Catholic University Press, 1952.

Manévy, Raymond. *La Presse de la Troisième République.* Paris: J. Foret, 1955.

Mermeix. *Le Ralliement et l'Action française*. Paris: A. Fayard, 1927.

Meyer, Arthur. *Ce que mes yeux ont vu*. Paris: Plon, Nourrit, 1911.

Miquel, Pierre. *L'Affaire Dreyfus*. Paris: P. U. F., 1959.

———— *Poincaré*. Paris: A. Fayard, 1961.

Montuclard, Maurice. "Aux Origines de la démocratie chrétienne," *Archives de Sociologie des Religions*, 6:47–89 (July–December 1958).

Moon, Parker T. *The Labor Problem and the Social Catholic Movement in France*. New York: Columbia University Press, 1921.

Muel, Léon. *Histoire politique de la septième législature*. Paris: Pedone, 1903.

Muret, Charlotte. *French Royalist Doctrines since the Revolution*. New York: Columbia University Press, 1933.

Naudet, Paul. *Pourquoi les catholiques ont perdu la bataille*. Paris: Foutemoing, 1904.

Osgood, Samuel M. *French Royalism under the Third and Fourth Republics*. The Hague: M. Nijhoff, 1960.

Payen, Fernand. *Poincaré chez lui*. Paris: Grasset, 1936.

Piou, Jacques. *Questions religieuses et sociales*. Paris: Plon, Nourrit, 1910.

———— *Le Ralliement, son histoire*. Paris: "Spes," 1928.

———— *Le Comte Albert de Mun, sa vie publique*. Paris: "Spes," 1919.

———— *D'Une guerre à l'autre 1871–1914*. Paris: "Spes," 1932.

Raphaël, Paul. *La République et l'église romaine de l'esprit nouveau à l'union sacrée*. Paris: J. Macé, 1948.

Rémond, René. *La Droite en France de 1815 à nos jours*. Paris: Aubier, 1954.

Rollet, Henri. *L'Action sociale des catholiques en France 1871–1901*. Paris: Boivin, 1947.

———— *Albert de Mun et le parti catholique*. Paris: Boivin, 1947.

Seignobos, Charles. *L'Évolution de la Troisième République*, Histoire de France contemporaine. Paris: Hachette, 1921.

Shapiro, David. "The Ralliement in the Politics of the 1890's," *The Right in France, 1890–1919*, David Shapiro, ed. London: Chatto & Windus, 1962.

Siegfried, André. *Tableau politique de la France de l'ouest*. Paris: A. Colin, 1913.

Soltau, Roger. *French Political Thought in the Nineteenth Century*. New York: Russell & Russell, 1959.

Soulier, A. *L'Instabilité ministérielle sous la Troisième République.*
    Paris: Sirey, 1939.
Tannenbaum, Edward R. *The Action Française.* New York: Wiley,
    1962.
Thibaudet, Albert. *Les Idées politiques de la France.* Paris: Stock,
    1932.
Tournier, J. *Le Cardinal Lavigerie et son action politique 1863–1892.*
    Paris: Perrin, 1913.
T'serclaes, Charles de. *Le Pape Léon XIII, sa vie, son action religi-
    euse, politique et sociale,* 2 vols. Paris: 1894.
Ward, James E. "Leo XIII and Bismarck; the Kaiser's Vatican Visit
    of 1888," *The Review of Politics,* 24:392–414 (July 1962).
—— "The French Cardinals and Leo XIII's *Ralliement* Policy,"
    Church History, 33:60–73 (March 1964).
Weber, Eugen. *Action Française.* Stanford, California: Stanford Uni-
    versity Press, 1962.
Weill, Georges. *Histoire du catholicisme libéral en France 1828–1908.*
    Paris: F. Alcan, 1909.
—— *Histoire de l'idée laïque en France au XIXe siècle.* Paris:
    F. Alcan, 1929.

INDEX

Abbés démocrates, 85
*Action catholique de la jeunesse fran-
  çaise,* 109
Adéodat, Abbé, 100
Alexander III, Tsar, 3, 47
Algiers, toast of, 109, 121, 123, 152,
  153
Alsace, Comte d', 78, 142, 146
Anticlericalism, 6, 9, 86, 90, 144, 151,
  159; in Italy, 2; of Opportunists in
  1880's, 25; debate over *droit d'acrois-
  sement,* 77–79
Anticlerical legislation, 17, 33, 55, 59,
  61, 75, 81, 86, 103, 110–112 *passim.,*
  120, 128, 132, 137, 141, 143, 145,
  147, 152, 155; Republican enactment
  of, 2; opposition of Left-Centrists to,
  22; during 880's, 25–26; *loi militaire,*
  26, 42, 43, 92, 116; *loi scolaire,* 42,
  43, 61, 103, 116, 121; *droit d'accroissement,* 77–79; *droit d'abbonne-
  ment,* 77, 82, 83, 134; Leo XIII's
  views on, 111; attitude of Assumptionists toward, 112; Jules Méline's
  views on, 48–49
Anti-Dreyfusards, 136
Anti-Semitism, 88, 95, 157
Arenberg, Prince d', 63, 69, 80
*Association catholique du commerce et
  de l'industrie,* 109
Association catholique française: formation of, in 1890, 43
*Association de la presse monarchique
  et catholique,* 31, 57
Association d l'Industrie, 35
Association Gambettiste, 140
Association laws of 1881, 88
Assumptionists, 55, 93, 97, 105, 106,
  108, 116, 155; attitude toward Third
  Republic, 87–88; cooperation with
  Étienne Lamy in 1896, 96; attitude
  toward Méline ministry, 103–104;

Lamy's complaints of, in 1897, 104–
  105; relations with Lamy in 1898,
  110; attitude toward anticlerical legislation, 112; influence in elections of
  1898, 116–117
Au milieu des sollicitudes, papal encyclical, 1892, 54, 56, 58, 65, 66, 85,
  124, 152, 153, 158; contents, 51–53;
  reaction of French Catholics to, 54–
  56; conservative reaction to, 56–58;
  reaction of *Droite constitutionnelle,*
  58–60
Austria-Hungary: diplomatic relations
  with Vatican, 2
Autorité, newspaper, 30

Bailly, Abbé, 96, 112
Bardoux, Henri, 22
Barthou, Louis, 76, 134, 137, 140, 143,
  147; speech at Oléron in 1898, 144–
  145
Béhaine, Lefebvre de, 8, 10, 54
Bélizal, Louis de, 16
Bellemayre, Comte de, 101, 115
Bishops, French Catholic, 84, 124; re-
  lations with the Republic, 9, 10; *droit
  d'abonnement* crisis, 79
Bismarck-Schoenhausen, Prince Otto
  von, 3
Bonaparte, Jerome, Prince, 12
Bonaparte, Eugène-Louis, Prince Im-
  perial, 12
Bonaparte, Victor, Prince, 12; attitude
  toward Boulangism, 20
Bonapartists, 18, 19, 25, 28, 30, 35, 36,
  71, 89, 114, 115, 123; and elections
  of 1881, 12
Bonjean, Jules, 43, 94, 108
Boulanger, Georges, 14, 20, 21, 25, 33,
  36, 120, 124
Boulangism, 28, 29, 30, 31, 37, 50, 82,

HARVARD HISTORICAL STUDIES